AF326517

*God's Guiding Light
Showed me the Way*

**A Memoir
by Richard Clayton Perdue**

God's Guiding Light
Showed Me the Way
A Memoir
by Richard Clayton Perdue

ISBN 13: 978-1-955338-40-0
Front cover and inside illustrations by Lori Graham
Book design and layout by Lori Graham
Printed in the United States of America

PP

POCAHONTAS PRESS

Floyd , VA
pocahontaspress.com

Preface

There are some people that say with age comes wisdom, but I don't agree with those people. I've met folks of all kinds. Foolish ones from ages 16 to 70. No, age doesn't make you any smarter, but living a long time does let you experience more, and let me tell you, I've experienced a lot in my life.

I've seen people live and seen people die. Some people change and others stay stubbornly the same. More than anything, I've seen life put me through the ringer with challenges that I didn't know how to face. But through it all I found a way to keep moving and never give up believing that the Lord had a purpose for me and my life.

If there's one thing I want you to take away from my experiences, its that no matter how bad you screw up or how hard things get, you can still make something of your life and make the world around you a better place.

Table of Contents

*God's Guiding Light
Showed Me the Way*

A Memoir
by Richard Clayton Perdue

CHAPTER 1:
First Birth

Everyone enters the world the same way and I was no different. Mommy told me that the night I was born she was lying in bed yelling out in pain while Dr. Newton, Sr. was in there with her smoking a big ol' cigar and singing "When the Roll is Called Up Yonder, I'll Be There." I never asked her if she enjoyed his singing that night, but I can't imagine she had asked for him to start. Regardless, I was born and was touched by the Lord's hand like all His creations.

I was Mommy and Daddy's first child; born on October 1st, 1949 to Annie Vance and Junor Clayton Perdue. Early on we lived in a little block house, sun-bleached yellow, made of only two rooms. The house had no electricity, no running water, and just an outhouse for a bathroom. Mommy and Daddy had done their part to make it more livable: Mommy had built a little garden outside, and Daddy had bought some animals such as chickens for meat and eggs, and pigs for sausage and ham. Some might find living like that hard to imagine, but for me and my kin this was the best we could do at the time. Water that you didn't get out of a well wasn't just a luxury, but an amenity far outside of our means.

Being an autumn baby meant one of the first seasons I really got to experience on earth was winter. Winter back then was intense, with snow almost up to your knees. As you can picture, a home without electricity meant a home without easy heating. I remember Daddy covering himself up with all the winter clothes he could and then wrapping his legs in cloth to trek outside into the snow, feeding the animals and getting firewood.

I didn't get to enjoy being an only child for long. My parents would end up having five children including myself, three boys and two girls. It wasn't uncommon for people to have big families then. More kids meant when they came of age there would be more hands to help with the house and to financially help support the family. Money was something that would always present a challenge for our family.

Daddy mostly worked as a farmhand to support all of us, and it was clear that it was a stressful situation for him. He had his problems, but supporting a family is not something that is easy. It took its toll on him.

The fact that we would have to move a lot wouldn't make things any easier. We lived in farmhouses, houses by the water, and little cabins. Some of them were nicer than others, but that didn't matter. We moved to where Daddy could find work.

Richard- Age 2

Of course, where we lived was also not important to a kid who didn't even understand how money worked yet. Like most people, memories of my young childhood are a bit blurry. Just the big incidents back then left an impression.

The earliest one of those memories that I can recall was with me and my cousin when I was around four years old. He and I were outside playing with a poleaxe. As I mentioned, having big families has its benefits, but it does make it hard to keep an eye on everyone at once. As my cousin was chopping dirt in that way only kids do when they are bored, I walked right in the path of his swing. The blade lodged in my head and when it was pulled out blood was flying everywhere.

Mommy and Daddy didn't have a car, so they had to ask our neighbor to take me to the doctor in town. After some debating with Daddy about how best to deal with me, the doctor stitched up my head. This wouldn't be the last time I had a passing brush with the reaper, but there was always a guardian angel looking out for me. Of course, some would just call that lucky, but the more it happened the more certain I was that I had a protector.

It wasn't too long after that head wound when I ended up finding a pack of delicious chocolates. Mommy started panicking, and I realized later I had eaten X-Lax. The doctors at the hospital had to put a tube up my nose to try and pump it out, but thankfully I saved them some time and threw it all up just after the tube had been put in. Daddy must have felt bad for me because on the ride back home he stopped and got me a toy truck. By then my first brother, Danny, was born and old enough to realize when he was getting left out, so after he started crying Daddy made me share my truck with him.

After we left the blockhouse, we wound up in a house with electricity. We could afford a radio for entertainment at that point, but nothing else. Of course, a radio is a whole lot more entertaining than nothing! On Saturday nights there would be barn dances broadcasted by the Grand Ole Opry, and we would tune in every week to listen. Mother Mabel Carter and Hank Williams were some of the performers I remember most. Entertainment was cheap then, but it still left you plenty happy. It was only once you had experienced more that you felt what you had wasn't good enough.

Following the birth of my sister Betty, we moved again to follow Daddy's work and with that we lost the electricity that we had become accustomed to. He started working for a doctor on his farm for 50 cents an hour, and around this same time I started school. I didn't last too long that first year. I caught whooping cough in the first month and my siblings caught it from me. Mommy decided that it was best for me to stay out of school while I recovered, so I got an extra year without having to worry about attending. Betty caught pneumonia around then too.

Daddy had lost so much sleep when she was in the hospital with pneumonia. I remember seeing him looking through small holes under the house and saying, "I know there is somebody in there." They ended up sending him to Marion's psychiatric hospital for a while; he had a nervous breakdown. Everyone had to work together to survive during this difficult time, but Mommy was a tough woman and kept us together.

During this time, I would run errands for Mommy. She would have me walk down to the general store, which was about a half mile away to get groceries for the family. Back then parents didn't worry so much about the safety of their kids. We knew everyone from around town, and you didn't hear about crimes unless they happened next door or happened to someone real important like the president. While I was running errands she would often can and dry food for storage, mostly for the winter season.

Of course, it wasn't all errands and easy living for me back then either. The doctor that Daddy worked for had a son of his own, two years older and two years bigger than me too. He had a nasty habit of picking on me when he was bored. He would tease me and hit me for his amusement.

One day, I got so fed up with it I asked Daddy if he could do something about it. He said to me, "Next time he picks on you, you pick something up and hit him back. That will teach him not to do that!" Of course, I had no reason to doubt Daddy's advice.

So, the next day when he and I were down by the creek and he started messing with me again, I waited until he stopped for a moment and was leaned down looking at something on the ground. I picked up a thick stick from the ground, came up behind him and smacked him hard against the back of the head with it! I don't know what I was expecting to happen, but I know I didn't expect blood to start spurting from his head and rushing down his face as he cried. I didn't know what to do so I took his hand and ran back home with him.

Mommy was able to get the bleeding stopped by putting a cold towel on his head. When Daddy got back from work, he worked up into a manic fuss. He told me I shouldn't have done that and that I had been bad. Daddy took off his belt and gave me a whipping. I knew he feared losing his job, but as far as I know the doctor didn't take it out on Daddy. The doctor's boy didn't play with me much after that.

By the time the next year came around, and I was ready to start school, Mommy had gotten pregnant again and Daddy had a new job which meant moving us into an old farmhouse. The house had been retrofitted with electricity, but not an indoor loo.

Daddy was still making 50 cents an hour, but it was around then when I started going to school that I learned that wasn't much money. Even before school, I noticed that each of us children only got two new pairs of pants a year, which was uncomfortable as we grew up. More noticeable was when Mommy would make my lunch every day for school, putting some of her homemade biscuits in my bag instead of sliced bread like the other school children. The kids would laugh at me because we couldn't afford sliced bread. I would try and hide my biscuit and eat it in my bag, but they still giggled about it. Looking back, it's an odd thing to tease someone about, but those little differences are the things kids notice. In a child's small world, a different type of bread can seem huge.

Of course, as the years passed it didn't take long for me to start dealing with bigger problems than what type of bread I had for lunch. By the time I had made it to the fourth grade, my sister, Violet, had been born and we had to move again. This time, Daddy went to work for Mommy's brother on a dairy farm in Bluefield, Virginia. It paid about the same but we got lots of food for free from the farm.

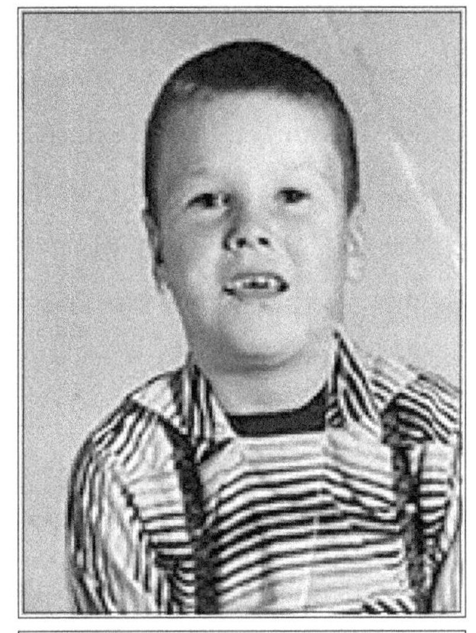

Richard- First Grade

It all seemed fine for a while until one day Daddy came home with a big lump on his neck. He and my uncle had gotten into a fight. My uncle had thumped Daddy hard on the neck with a stick and Daddy said he was never going back. Of course, that meant we would have to move again. Hard to justify living on the property where you had just quit working

Daddy went to work at another dairy farm back in Giles County, and we ended up living in an old farmhouse where the Carillon Giles Hospital sits today. Between moving houses Mommy had my youngest brother, Ronnie. That made us a family of seven in total.

Mommy and Daddy started to fuss and argue a lot when we moved this time. I was already ten, but I had the hardest time figuring out what the arguments were about.

Richard- Seventh Grade

Daddy would just come in from work in the evening and start fussing.

Then one day, Daddy was home for lunch and argued with Mommy again. I tried not to listen to it when I could avoid it. When Daddy had left and was headed back to work, Mommy told me to sneak down the hill and find someone at the service station. She wanted them to call the police and tell them that Daddy had threatened to kill her. I had no idea. I knew they had argued, and I knew Daddy had problems in the past, but I was shook hearing her tell me that. Of course, I did as I was told and went down there to have them call the police. By that afternoon, they had arrested Daddy and taken him off to jail.

Mommy was upset, recounting what had happened so many times to anyone who would listen. I wanted to help her and do what I thought was right, so when Daddy's trial arrived, I said I had heard Daddy say he was going to kill her. After I said that Daddy got sent to the mental ward again.

The truth is I wasn't sure if I did hear that or not. I didn't truly know. I knew I wanted to help Mommy, but not knowing if I was telling the truth up there on the stand weighed on me something terrible. Even now, when it was so long ago, I still wonder if I did the right thing or not. Right or wrong, I did it, and now our house was a family of six instead of seven.

With Daddy in the mental ward again, we had no reason to live where we were anymore. Mommy had us move to a rental house in Wayside. She didn't have a job, so we were living off of social welfare checks. We bought a television; It was the first one we ever had. In 1960, it was a good source of entertainment for a kid my age, and a change of pace from just the radio. At night time, I loved watching television.

I don't know whether Mommy was genuinely relieved not to have Daddy around with his mood swings or if she was just trying really hard to make everything feel good and normal, but she would dote on us kids a lot more. The year Daddy went to jail; she got me the best Christmas gift I had ever received: a new red bicycle. It still brings back good memories when I think about it now, so I suppose she did succeed in making everything feel good back then.

That all being said, we weren't cut off from Daddy, and Mommy hadn't abandoned him. We would visit him sometimes, having someone with a car drive us all down there to see him in Marion. It never felt good seeing him knowing I had help put him there, but he didn't seem to hold a grudge about what I had said.

It happened again, while Daddy was away, a neighborhood kid started to pick on me. Boys back then were rowdy and always looking for an outlet for their energy. I remember some of the boys, when they were bored, would start throwing whatever was on hand at each other: rocks or apples mostly. One day when this boy started picking on me with his sister there, I finally snapped and fought back. I knocked him to the ground and sat on top of him, choking him. I had no intention of stopping just because he was on the ground, but his sister got a broom and smacked me as hard as she could at the top of my head with the handle. It was for the best. I was too angry to stop without some intervention, but it left me with a big egg-shaped lump on my head.

Daddy also started to do more with us boys. Since we lived close to the New River at that time, he would take us fishing a fair amount. My brothers and I would also look for discarded soda bottles along the banks of the river. If we brought them back into town, we could get two cents for each one. That's how we would buy ourselves candy.

Life wasn't always easy then, but it didn't seem so bad when compared to the past. We had nothing like the Civil War happening in our country nor sending men away like World War II. Daily activities became a lot safer too. For one, motor vehicles were a lot less jumpy than horses. In fact, my Grand-Daddy was killed at Rich Creek by a team of horses. He was plowing snow one day; he always plowed with the check lines for the horses around his neck. He was close to the tracks on the Virginian Railroad when a train came by. He waved at the train because he didn't want them to blow the whistle, one of his horses was skittish. The engineer blew the horn anyway, and it scared

Richard- Junior High

the horses. They ran off and Grand-Daddy fell off the cart. The lines around his neck meant he couldn't get loose from the horses dragging him into the turning plow. It went through his stomach and tore the side of his head off.

Getting hit in the head with an axe as a little boy did not seem so bad after hearing about tragedies like that

CHAPTER 2:
Teenage Antics and Young Love

By 1963, I had graduated from Rich Creek Elementary School and was ready to start the fall semester at Narrows High School. The school had been built just that year. During that time, we moved again, this time up into the mountains. It was just us up there; our nearest neighbor was over half a mile away. The house was incomplete, with the bedrooms upstairs only having studs and nothing else. One day my youngest brother, Ronnie, was upstairs jumping on one of the beds for fun. Apparently, he took too big of a leap as he jumped right off the bed. He smashed through the wall and fell down through the ceiling of the living room and landed in the floor in front of Mommy who was ironing some clothes. They took him to the doctor, and he had to get three clamps under his chin.

Even with the house in that state, I came to like it a lot up there, in part because I had started taking a liking to hunting around then. Mommy had bought me a Remington single shot .22 rifle from the hardware store for 18 dollars, and with all the woods around us, I was using it a lot.

I loved the mountains, and I'll admit that my love for them was a bit blinding at times. My grades weren't too good in school because I would often daydream in class, and my stint on the football team was mighty short, as it took away from my squirrel hunting time.

What also took away from that time was that Daddy said I had become old enough to start working. I would help him plow the fields at his job, something I hated to do in the heat, and I would help Daddy with the side jobs he would do to make some extra money. He would raise pigs and slaughter them for the meat; one for our family, and a few others to sell for extra money. He and I also would cut black locust trees to make posts to sell for a dollar each in town. We would have to carry them down the mountain on our backs; we still didn't have a car and we didn't have neighbors to ask to drive us anymore. Daddy never gave me any money to help with that.

During that time, I would also look after my grandmother at her house on the weekends. I would get her wood and coal she needed to last her all week. It was about a mile walk to her house on Fridays from school. She appreciated me being there. Often, it would just be me and her there as she didn't have many guests. I also delivered her supplies, and she would give me money so that I could do something fun on the weekend or buy my lunch for the next week. She made good money working at the Celanese factory as a janitor. When I would come there, she would fix a meal that would make someone think there were about 20 people coming for dinner. I would eat until I was about to pop, yet grandma would say, 'You'd better eat! You haven't eaten hardly anything."

Eventually, Daddy made enough money to buy a two wheel Gravely tractor. He later traded the tractor to my first cousin, Howard, for a 1957 Desoto car with a- push button transmission. We didn't need to carry those posts down from the mountains by hand then, and had a way to get around other than our own two feet.

Daddy certainly treated me differently as I grew older. I remember one time he asked me to come over to him as he was reading the bible. He tried to get me to read along with him, and at the time I didn't understand why. He was also talking about seeing the Grim Reaper in the sky. Now I understand he had conviction and wanted to show me something he had found in himself in that book, but his words about the reaper make me wonder what he exactly hoped me to learn that day.

I still had hunting too much on the mind to care what he was saying back then and started enjoying it even more when Elmer Fleeman and his wife Betty moved into a house up on the mountain near us. Not only did we have a neighbor, but I had a hunting partner in Elmer. With Elmer watching over me we started coon hunting in the night. He was an enjoyable man to have around, easygoing. One night while hunting he gave me my first beer. I really thought I was something special after that. It's almost laughable now.

One time Elmer and I were out hunting at night on the mountain. We would use a kerosene lamp to help us see, which wasn't all that good at lighting things up, but we were walking a path we knew well enough while looking for game. I was moving the light around looking for some raccoons with Elmer behind me, when I turned around a tree and was staring right into a big pair of eyes! It gave me such a horrible fright that I fell to the ground and dropped the lantern. Elmer had seen it all, and he was laughing hard. Around that tree, I had almost run into an owl sitting on a tree branch. I was shaking, worked up into such a fright and also now a bit embarrassed. I stood up and shouted, "I'm never going hunting ever again!"

I was back out there as soon as I got home from school the next day.

*****

I wasn't a good student at school, but now that we had settled into living in one place for a bit, I made some friends. Unsurprising for teenage boys, we were a rowdy bunch that could stir up some trouble when we got going.

On Halloween night of our sophomore year, we came up with the idea that we would cut some trees down across the road so we wouldn't have to go to school the next day. The days before Halloween we found the trees we were going to cut. We got a crosscut saw and an ax ready. As soon as it got dark, we started.

We must have cut about ten trees.

We thought for sure that we were getting out of going to school the next day. To our dismay, the next morning there was a hole cut through the trees big enough for the bus to get through. The highway department had come in at midnight and foiled our plans.

There was this feeling that we all wanted to impress each other. We would drink beer, chew tobacco, and do anything else we could to be something to each other. Once one of us did it, we all would be doing it before long. I figure I felt that more than anyone else. I thought I was lower than everybody else because my family didn't have as much. I had to work just to pay for my school lunches. When I was sixteen, I got a job cleaning an office building after school. While other kids had money from their parents, I had to work for myself, only occasionally having a little bit extra left over when I was done.

When I had that little bit of extra money, we would all go to Rich Creek on Saturday night to the movies. I had to walk about two miles off the mountain and then hitchhike to Rich Creek. I had to do the same thing coming back too. I liked to go and watch all the Elvis Presley movies, and enjoyed them a lot, but, boy, it was a long walk coming back up that mountain in the dark.

Also, on Saturday nights, since I lived up in the mountains, there would be all sorts of young people that would come up there for some intimate privacy. My friends and I would sneak out there at night. There would always be someone parked down at the end of our driveway thinking it was just an empty road. Of course, boys will be boys. We would always listen to what was happening in those cars, trying to stifle our laughing. Oh, the things we heard!

Girls are on just about every boy's mind at that age, and I was no different. I was seventeen when I met my dream girl. I was standing in the hallway one day and I saw the most beautiful girl I had ever seen walking down the hall. She was an eighth grader. I thought in my mind that she had to be mine. This idea though seemed so foolish. She was too pretty to want a guy like me. I didn't know who she was, but I didn't want to give up on her.

I was standing at my locker one day right beside Bill Purdue's locker, when I saw her walking down the hallway. I said, "there comes my dream girl," and Bill asked me who I was talking about. I pointed her out to him. He said, "That's my sister." It was true. That was his sister Carolyn. He wasn't as friendly to me after that.

Word got around in school that I liked her. She didn't act like she was interested in me, but romance at that age is funny. There was another girl in her class that had a crush on me, and that girl started talking about how much she wanted to be with me. I guess she must have brought up some good points because Carolyn started liking me after a while. I began speaking to her and eventually we started hanging out and walking around the halls together. Somehow, at some point, that made us a couple.

*****

When my senior year came around, I was so excited because Daddy had arranged a job for me at the nursing home in town where he had been working. I would be going to school for half a day then working from 3 pm to 11 pm at the nursing home. I worked six days a week and would use my money to take Carolyn to the movies when I hitchhiked to Narrows. I was so excited to have a job, but even more than

front row (from left): Betty, Ronnie, Violet
back row: Danny, Daddy, Mommy, Richard

that I was excited that my eighteenth birthday was coming up. Daddy would not sign for me to get my driver's license, so I had to wait until I was eighteen. I would be eighteen on October first and I could practically taste the freedom that would come with being able to drive.

It took me all three attempts I was allowed, but I got my license. I was over the moon! Of course, I didn't have a car yet, and Daddy didn't let me use the truck much but all I had to do was save up some money and I would have a car of my own. The only problem was that saving up money is tough when you're spending most of it as soon as you make it. I was disheartened.

This one special old man in the nursing home though, made my life for the better in more ways than one. He was very friendly and when I finished my work at night, I would go to his room, sit and talk. He really enjoyed it, and I enjoyed having someone to talk to late at night as well.

One night he asked me what I would like to have more than anything else. I told him there was a 1955 Ford car across the river at Akers Motor Company. I had been looking at the car and would love to have it. He asked how much it cost. I told him $200. That was all that was said about it. About a week later, I went into his room one night and sat down. He held out his hand and said here and handed me some money. I asked, "What is that?" The man said take this and go get that car you like and keep it to yourself. He was a retired owner of a coal company in West Virginia, and he had money.

I thanked him and could have jumped for joy. No one had ever given me anything like that before. I went out and bought that car the next day. I got the tags and insurance and was on cloud nine. I could go anywhere I wanted now.

Probably to be expected, later on, his boy asked him what he did with the money, and I guess he kept after him until he told him. His son went to the administrator of the nursing home and complained about it. They weren't too happy to hear I had taken money from someone living there, and they said they would make arrangements for me to pay it all back. They would deduct a certain amount every pay day from my check. Mr. Coleman passed away though, and they never did deduct any money from my check.

The administrators must not have been that upset. There were two or three other men at the nursing home that asked me to take them for a ride in my car. I asked the administrator if I could drive them around town. He said yes, but I would need to get permission from their families. I would take them for a ride every day, and the family would pay me. I was actually making more money than Daddy was. It was amazing to have that car.

For a while I had a good thing going for me, but of course everything being that nice was fragile. Far more fragile than I realized back then. One day I decided to lay out of school, something I would do when I was feeling particularly adventurous and very bored. I went and picked up a friend of mine, Larry, and we drove over to West Virginia. Over there the age to buy alcohol was only eighteen and we were primed to abuse that fact.

We bought two cases of beer, and we started guzzling it down and feeling good about it. Just to show off how above it all we were, we went in front of the high school and started burning rubber with the car. Just puffing out our chests to show off. We then went to Peterstown to the high school and lay tracks there too. We wanted everyone to know how much fun we were having.

We decided to go to Ballard and get my first cousin, then go to Roanoke and prowl around. We went back down to the main road and started towards Ballard out Route 12. As we were going through a straight stretch, a 1964 Chevy Impala passed us like we were sitting still. When he blew past us, I mashed the gas pedal to the floor and then caught up with him as we went into the first curve. I looked at the speedometer, and I was doing 90 miles an hour. I never let off the gas pedal. When I got in the middle of the curve, I ran off the shoulder of the road, pulled the car back on to the road, and then went into a spin. I don't know how many times we turned, but then the car rolled over the bank. I guess I passed out. When I came to, my car was facing the same way we had been going from the start. Larry had been thrown some distance down through the yard. Seatbelts back then were barely thought of as necessary so that kind of stuff could happen easily.

The car was planted in front of the front porch of a house. Kids had been playing in the yard, but now they were watching me. When I got out of the car, other people came over too, curious to see what happened. I barely realized what had just occurred and thought they just wanted to have some fun. I told the people if they wanted the beer, to get it and take it out of there. They must have wanted to have some fun, because the beer was gone in just a few minutes.

They took Larry out in an ambulance. He was knocked out. I wasn't hurt at all, but I was still a drunken fool.

With the ambulance came the town police. The officer there told me that he had seen me up at the high school spinning around and showing off. He told me that the state police wouldn't be there for two to three hours, so he took me up to his house and made a pot of coffee. The officer made me drink several cups of coffee. He got enough coffee in me to seem like I wasn't drunk, and he said we better go back down there before the state police arrived.

Once back to the wrecked vehicle, I put a big chew of tobacco in my mouth. The state police came and didn't even give me a ticket. It's real hard to believe that not any one person mentioned the beer, but I guess they didn't want to make any trouble. That was definitely the best for me.

I got a wrecker to tow my car back to our house. Every inch of the car was smashed up. This was an era when cars were made to be tough, made from things like steel, but every bit of it was mangled-the body, the wheels, even the motor mounts were broken loose. It was a miracle that both of us survived.

Two of my friends came that evening and wanted me to go to Radford, a nearby town less than an hour away. They wanted to go see two girls, and it sounded like fun to me. The idea of thinking about what had happened didn't cross my mind. My mind still had some alcohol affecting my decision making. It was very late that night when we got home.

The next morning, when I looked at that car I had wanted so badly, it made me feel sick. It was unrepairable even if I had the money. I would have had a nervous fit if the man who had bought it for me was still alive. It was my big ticket to freedom, and it was now nothing more than scrap. I had planned on taking Carolyn to the prom in it, but now I was back to walking and hitchhiking. My car was gone.

You might think that getting drunk and destroying something you cherished so much might make a boy think of how to change his behavior, but the boy would need to be able to self-reflect and want to change. I will admit self-reflection was not a high priority when I was young.

On the day of prom, my friend Roger Jennings and I took his car into West Virginia and to a creek so we could clean it up. He had agreed to take me to the prom, but I had yet to learn my lesson. I stopped and got some beer to drink while we washed his car. Well, it wasn't some beer. It was enough for me to pass out in our front yard when I got home. If it hadn't been for Mommy getting me cleaned up, I would have missed my senior prom in its entirety. When I got to the prom I was dressed, but still plenty drunk. Carolyn could smell the beer on me. I tried to lie to her and tell her I hadn't been drinking, but she didn't believe me. Here I was four years older than her and yet about ten years less mature. She was disappointed, but she stayed with me. I guess she loved me.

When it came time to graduate, I only barely made it there in one piece, by the grace of God. I was a mess. No one from my family came to the graduation. I suppose you can make that what you will. I guess they knew if I didn't care about it much, they had no reason to either.

By November 1968, my first fall after graduation, I didn't have a job and I was broke. My best friend Alvin and my brother Danny decided we were going on a camping trip on top of Peters Mountain. I had nothing better to do and deer season opened on Monday. We decided to leave on Sunday so that we would be there and ready once it opened. We had never done anything like this, but we were about 10 to 12 miles away from home, so it didn't seem crazy to spend the night up there in preparation.

We took Alvin's jeep, with a plan of what we would do when we got there. We cut some small trees down and built a frame for a shelter to stay in. Using clear plastic, we covered the frame. We had a door, but the nest was basically airtight. Although we didn't have sleeping bags, we had blankets to cover up with. For heat, we had a kerosene heater to keep us warm and a propane gas lamp for light. Looking back, this was probably one of the dumbest things I ever did in my life. Three boys sleeping in an airtight shelter made of plastic with a kerosene heater burning inside. It is a miracle of God that we all didn't die from a fire or asphyxiation, but we were fine. We laid there that night and listened to the deer walking around outside, just waiting for tomorrow.

Up the next morning before daylight, none of us could wait to start the day. We ate our breakfast and went hunting. Sometime that day between the three of us, we killed a buck. After bringing it back to the campsite, we threw a rope over a tree limb and pulled the deer up high enough so that animals couldn't get to it. Only one buck wasn't enough for us though, so we went back to sleep in our nest, ready to find more the next day.

That night, it started to snow. By the time we got up the next morning, it had snowed about 12 inches. We stayed that day and decided that the next day we would go home. The snow slowed us down though, so we didn't find anything that day.

The next morning, we went to start the jeep. Turned the key and nothing. It wouldn't start. There we were, 12 miles from home on top of Peters Mountain, 12 inches of snow on the ground, and a deer hanging in a tree.

We only had one choice, walk home. We could then get someone to come that had a jeep and could jump start Alvin's jeep. Cell phones hadn't been invented, and we didn't have any way to communicate with the rest of the world. We got our guns and started our journey home, walking all day through the snow in the cold. Right after sunset, we made it. It was an exhausting trek home and felt like a waste of our time. Alvin got Merle Hedrick to take his jeep and drive us to our camping spot. This trip made me realize something important: I needed a job and to go back to work.

Carolyn and Richard-High School

CHAPTER 3:
Dancing with the Devil

Once I started looking for work, it wasn't long before I found a job. I heard from chatting around that the Hercules Radford Army Ammunition Plant was hiring. I hitched a ride with someone over there and applied. I filled out an application, took all the tests, and they hired me right then and there. I went to work the next day, making $3.25 an hour, the most I had ever made. Work was easier to find back then.

The job required working shift work, but it didn't matter to me. I had a job and soon I'd have money. The only problem was, I had to find a ride over there. I was riding with my first cousin, Jimmy Carter, who was a few years older than me, but I didn't like having to rely on him like that.

The first day I went to work, I was working in a cutting house on the A-Line, where they cut the powder. The powder had a lot of alcohol, 190 proof, and from that proof, ether floated into the air. I was breathing it the whole time I worked, so by the end of that first night, I felt like I was half drunk. The first few days are always the worst in a new job, but I fit in pretty good, and my body adapted to the fumes after a few days.

Soon I had my first paycheck, and I knew what I wanted to get with it: a ride. Along with needing to hitch around, I had been borrowing Daddy's Mercury to take Carolyn out on our dates. It was not ideal for a teenage boy. I remember one time, Carolyn and I went parking up in the mountains above Peterstown in a field under a big oak tree. It came a bad thunderstorm, but it didn't bother us. We were too busy to notice it. I tell you, if Daddy had caught us up there in his Mercury, he wouldn't have let me step foot in his car again!

I went to the Ford garage in Pearisburg to look for a car. They had a 1956 Ford Victoria in pink and black. I just had to have it. It was like new, I just fell in love with it. Carolyn liked it too, so now we had a ride. I was very happy—I had a job, I had a car, and I had the prettiest girl in the world—I was in love!

My life was lining up real nicely, but that didn't mean I respected what I had. Like most young kids, if you are not really careful, the devil will take you down a road you don't need to go.

Not long after I bought the Victoria, Roy Fletcher bought some school buses and started a bus service to haul people to work and back. He ran the buses three shifts a day, seven days a week. I started riding the bus to work since it cost $1 a day—you couldn't drive it for that. It was a smart business he had.

You could also give him your order for alcohol when you went to work, and he would have what you wanted when you got off work. That wasn't a smart idea.

We would drink almost every night when we were working the 4pm-12am shift. It meant our commute bus was also a bar, and I wasn't the only one who was a customer. One night I was working from 12am-8am, and a guy came into work drunk. One job we were doing required workers to pull powder out of a piece of equipment called a macerator-grinding machine. We were supposed to shut it down and pull the powder out of it into ten-gallon stainless steel tubs. Then it would go to the blockers to be pressed into cubes. This guy didn't shut the vessel off, and he tried to pull the powder out with it running. He got the brass rake hung in the blades inside the equipment. It locked up.

The equipment was full of powder and the belt kept running then started burning and smoking. Everyone who worked there knew that a single flame could blow the place to kingdom come. When the macerator started shaking, I knew it was going to blow. It scared me to death. I dashed out the door and just started running. I didn't stop until I was over the hill near the armory.

By some miracle, it didn't destroy the whole place in a fireball. The safety department came and said the powder was fired, but then it smothered out. Looking back now, I realize that what really happened was an act of God. God smothered out the fire—He wasn't through with me. I didn't realize it then, but God had planned a long journey ahead for me.

You would think a drunk man almost burning me alive might scare me away from alcohol, but I wasn't that smart or just too stubborn to push me away from something I enjoyed. One night, we were working 4pm – 12am, and when we got off work, Jimmy had a pint jar of moonshine. We drank that on the way home. When we got to Rich Creek, we got in my car and decided to go get something else to drink. We drank a couple more hours. Jimmy was driving my car. He drove up to his house above Peterstown, got out, and let me have my car. I was plenty drunk by the time I had taken the wheel. I started toward home, but I passed where I was supposed to turn off and decided to keep going. Driving through Peterstown and then turning, I drove towards the cemetery that sat above the town. As I started up that gravel road, I began to lose control of the vehicle. I mashed the accelerator down, hoping it would level out, but instead it just started spinning. I skidded out of the road.

When the car stopped, it was sitting at an awkward angle. I couldn't see anything but was pretty sure I had run it into a ditch. I let the clutch out to see if I could move the car, but it didn't budge. I decided to get out and see just how stuck I was. Stepping out of the car, I tried to walk around it, but only started falling. And falling. And falling.

I fell probably 200 to 300 feet down. Rocks cut up my skin, my shoes flew off, I smashed my leg badly, and by the time I had stopped moving, blood was running down my face. I had no idea what to do except get back to my car, so I started crawling. After much effort, I finally reached the rise of the bank. The car had two tires sitting on the road, and two tires sitting just plain in the air. The passenger side of the car was completely off the ground, supported by nothing but the other half of the car.

Even drunk, I had the good sense to walk home after seeing that. It seemed like it took forever as I stumbled down the road and out of town. Eventually I made it to the house, and I beat on the door, hollering for Mommy to let me in. I was covered with blood, filthy, and had worn the bottoms out of my socks. Finally, a woman came to the door, but it wasn't Mommy, and she ran me off screaming. I was at the wrong house. We used to live at this home of the now occupied and wailing woman, but now we lived about three miles away.

Once I realized my mistake, I kept walking. The sun was coming up when I got home. It terrified Mommy when she saw me. She got me cleaned up and fixed me some breakfast. Daddy questioned me about what happened and where the car was. I told him where I thought it was, and he said we better go and see what shape it was in and figure out what we should do.

Daddy and I drove by the cemetery and then saw my car up ahead, still sitting there. As we approached the scene, Daddy walked over and looked at the car hanging over the bank. At the bottom of the drop off sat a swift-moving creek. In that moment, he broke down and started crying like a baby. That was the only time in my life that I ever saw my Daddy cry. I suppose he realized how close I was to meeting my Maker. I still barely could believe I had fallen down that bank myself.

We got a wrecker to come and get the car back on the road. The side was bent up, but it was still drivable, so I still had transportation. I was skinned up badly, and I had a significant limp. I went to the doctor and was told that nothing was broken but missed work that night. The following night when I returned to work, pushing powder on a wagon from the mix house to the blockers and on my feet the whole shift hurt like crazy, but I made it through.

My Daddy - Junior Clayton Perdue

CHAPTER 4:
Property of Uncle Sam

In April, I was still working at the ammunition plant. When I pulled the 4-12 pm shift, I always stopped at the post office in Rich Creek and got the mail. On this particular day, I had a letter from the Selective Service. "Congratulations! You have been selected to serve in the Armed Forces of the United States of America," the letter read. Seeing that sent chills through my body. I could have cried.

Earlier in the year, I had received a letter that instructed me to report to Roanoke and take an Army physical exam. It wasn't long before I was given a classification of 1-A. At that time, when you got a 1-A classification, it was just a matter of time until you were called to active duty.

That time had come. I was supposed to report for duty in June. I went to work and gave them my notice. They wanted me to work until I had to leave, but I wasn't having any of that. I was going to quit now and party it up until the time I had to go, I informed them. I didn't know if I would ever be back or not. The Vietnam War was going strong by then. Getting drafted could be a death sentence. A lot of young boys went to Canada to keep from going. I wasn't going to run, but I was sure going to enjoy my time before I had to go.

I started my partying and got drunk. And then I stayed drunk. I was drinking every day I could, which made it easier to not think about what might happen in the future. One day a Marine Corps recruiter came by my house to talk to me. He said if you join the Marines, you can stay home 30 more days before you have to leave. That sounded like a good idea to me. More time at home meant more time I could keep enjoying my life and Carolyn. Everyone told me that I was crazy to do that, that Marines saw tons of action in the war, but now I didn't have to leave until July—and I had another month to party.

Unsurprisingly, given how much I was drinking, I had another wreck. A car hit me in the rear end and tore the vehicle up. I was still able to drive it, but now the rear end and the side were both mashed up and it was looking pretty sad.

When July came around, my family had a cookout for me before I left at the Cascades Park in Pembroke. We took plenty of beer. I enjoyed beer so much, and my dad was there staying sober. He had quit drinking years ago. I kept pushing him to drink a beer with me, he said no several times, but eventually he relented. Maybe my dad wanted to do something for his son as he was going away. I have wished a thousand times that I had never done that to him, but I did and he had that beer with me and with that he started drinking again. The time flew by, and soon it was time for me to go.

*****

I had a long way to go before they could even train me, much less go to war. First, I had to go to the Beckley, West Virginia Induction Center for processing. A Greyhound bus picked up the draftees and shuttled us to Beckley, where we were put up in a hotel for the night. The next morning, we were all sworn in and then loaded into a Greyhound bus again for Charleston, West Virginia, en-route to the airport. Next stop, Parris Island, South Carolina -- the basic training location for the Marine Corps.

The Marines flew their people everywhere they had to go when they changed duty stations. I had never flown before, and I'd say most of the other boys had never flown either. They loaded us on a jet, and the guy I was sitting next to was very pale. We started down the runway, and I watched the terminal as we went past it, then at the face of the guy sitting next to me. Now his face was as red as blood.

I liked flying. We moved fast and with a nice view out the window. What wasn't to like? We flew to Atlanta and we had a layover to change flights to go to Charleston, South Carolina. I sat at the window and watched as we flew over a thunderstorm. It amazed me to see lightening jump from one cloud to another. I hadn't ever seen anything like that. The wonders of our Lord's nature at work never ceased to amaze me.

When we landed and came down the steps from the jet, there was a short guy in a uniform. He had one of those hats like the ranger in yogi bear would wear on his head, except he was yelling and screaming. I had never heard anything like that. Every other word that came out of his mouth was a curse word. He made us sit in the lobby and wait on another flight coming in. He called us everything but a child of God. The other flight landed so they put us all on Greyhound buses once again for the final leg of our trip to Parris Island.

Someone opened a window on the bus that I was in, and that really made

Boot camp at Parris Island

the man in charge mad. They threatened to take anybody who opened a window to the brig when we got there. We finally arrived at Parris Island. The buses stopped. The door on the bus opened, and what came through the door would scare anyone to death—especially a bus full of 18- and 19-year-old boys. I thought to myself, "They are right. I am crazy. I stayed home 30 more days for this? I've got to be crazy!"

The drill instructor (DI) was screaming and hollering like a plum idiot, not that anyone in the bus was going to tell him. I'd never seen anyone scream like that. We were told to exit the bus and stand in the footprints in the parking lot. When we got off the bus there were even more DIs screaming just as loud as the one we had! They were everywhere.

They lined us up for our haircuts. I looked at the ones in front of me, already in the barber chairs. Most of them had long hair, they looked like they could cry. My hair was long and combed back over my head, much like Elvis's style.

We were issued uniforms and a bag of toiletry items such as toothpaste and a toothbrush. We were told to hold on to what we were given, and we had better not lose it. If you sat anything down somebody would get it, and you didn't have any choice but get another wherever you could find it.

We spent the whole night getting all our government-issued items and clothing. This was the scariest night I have ever spent in my life. I had no idea what to expect, but I knew my expectations were nothing like this reality. I thought the day would never end.

Finally, daylight came and we were marched to breakfast--they called it chow. I couldn´t eat it. I was used to mama´s cooking and I thought I wouldn´t give this to the pigs to eat. I had not eaten since the day before at breakfast. I was hungry but not enough to eat that stuff.

After breakfast we were assigned to platoons, each having sixty people. We spent that first day getting settled in and organized. We were shown how to make up a sack. I knew how to make a bed, after working at a nursing home during my senior year of high school.

The senior DI told us that we were now the property of Uncle Sam, and what was expected from us.

The July temperature in South Carolina hit a high of about 100 degrees and we were hot and exhausted. Finally, the instructors allowed us to hit the sack at 9 pm. I had been drinking and partying for the past three months. It was a mighty big change. I would lay there in my bed that night and hear people sobbing all over the barracks. I finally went to sleep.

At 5 am the next morning, I woke to the sound of a trashcan falling through the barracks and the DI yelling at the top of his voice. We had to get up and stand out in front of our sack, dressed only in our undershorts and t-shirts. The instructor said to take our sheets off our bed and hold them in front of us for inspection. As the DI circled like a shark, I was so proud the night before because I had made my bed up so nice. It made me feel like a right fool for that hard work only to have it torn up. I didn´t know at the time why they did that, but it was to see if anyone had wet the bed. They wanted to whip anyone who did that further into shape. Of course, once that was done, we had to make the bed again.

We had to go on a one-mile run that day. As a man that had been drunk for three months and the temperature over 90 degrees, I thought I was going to die! My stomach felt ready to burst and my lungs were on fire. I saw two guys drop out and then witnessed what happened to them. The DIs beat them with sticks while they were walking. I made myself a vow: I would never drop out even if it killed me. I guess that was the attitude they wanted to instill in everybody. If that was the case, it sure worked for me.

I guess the movie *Full Metal Jacket* is the closest thing I've seen to the boot camp experience. I'm sure plenty of people thought that was exaggerated, but that was pretty close to the way boot camp really was. Believe me though, it was a lot worse in person than the movie.

One day a messenger came from the battalion headquarters and said that I had a phone call. I couldn't even imagine who could be calling me. I would not have thought that would even be possible. I picked up the phone and it was Carolyn. Her brother Bill had been killed in a car wreck. Bill was the same age as me and hadn't approved of us, but it still was a shock to hear that. There were three of them in the car. Bill and Steve Beasley, and Jerry Clark - he was driving and the only one to survive. It hurt but there was nothing I could do. It was out of the question for me to go home.

We learned everything about Marine Corps life. We had 30 minutes of free time every night. We typically used this time to write a letter home, read our mail, take care of our gear, take a shower and use the bathroom. No one liked it but they were changing us from boys to men. We stayed busy all the time: classes, marching, and physical training. The Marine DIs taught us to march and move as a platoon. Every move was exactly at the same time. On Sundays, everyone went to church. Catholics went to one service, and Protestants went to another.

Recruits had an obstacle course we had to go through. One part of the course required climbing about 30 feet in the air. There was a rope that went down at an angle. We had to go down the rope feet first and then headfirst. One-third of the way down, we had to change and go headfirst, and then go another third and change back to feetfirst. It had a big pool of water underneath. If someone slipped, they would fall into the water and had to start over again until they could make it.

Sometimes we would have to stand in formation and scream "Kill, kill, kill!" They were trying to break us. If someone was going to crack, they would rather that an individual breakdown in bootcamp instead of combat. They told us that the waters around Parris Island had piranha in them in case anybody wanted to try to leave. I didn't know at the time, but piranha are not in North America. Not a single one of us in that platoon wanted to test it to see if they were telling the truth. We also learned about the military code of justice and were issued our rifles.

It came time that we had to go to the rifle range for two weeks. I thought to myself this will be a breeze. I had hunted all my life and had shot guns. We lived in the Appalachian Mountains, and I figured I knew it all. I was so wrong. Turns out what we had been doing in the mountains was nothing more than having fun with guns. We had to learn exactly how to hold our M-14, squad positions we had to get in, and how to put the sling in our arms. They would make us stay in position, making sure we didn't break, and it hurt a lot to do that.

It was a hard thing to deal with, and some deal with it worse than others. One morning a guy in another platoon had slipped a round into his pocket. That morning he put the round in the chamber and put the rifle under his chin and pulled the trigger.

The second week of rifle training we were divided in half. Half would shoot and half would work the butts. The butts are where the targets are located, and the task involved running the targets up and down so the shooter and the DI could see where he had hit the target.

My thoughts about how to shoot didn't work out well. They claimed it was easier to train someone to shoot that had never fired a gun. That really tore my technique all to pieces. I was rooted in my way of shooting a gun, I will admit it. So, one day Sgt. Malone pulled me off the firing line and took my M-14. He locked the bolt back and told me to stick my trigger finger into the chamber. I did and he pushed the release and let the bolt go home on my finger. It was like laying your finger on an anvil and someone hitting it with a hammer. Pain like you couldn't believe. I was always a very stubborn individual. He asked me if it hurt, and I said no. He said put it in there again. I wouldn't have told him it hurt if it killed me. He released the bolt and it smashed my finger again. He asked if it hurt again. Oh, it hurt a lot, but you better believe I said no. He said to put my finger in there again and let the bolt go home again and the blood flew out. He got a Band-Aid and put it on my finger.

He told me "You don´t tell anyone what I have done". They don't like to show it, but even the drill instructors have lines they aren't supposed to cross, and apparently drawing blood was a red line.

Needless to say, I didn´t qualify. I was sent back to another platoon and had to shoot another week. I still didn´t qualify.

The next week we had mess duty and had to go to the Woman Marine Battalion to work. We were told if you get caught looking at one of them you will be taken to the Brig. We couldn´t even speak to them.

The next week, we had to go to Elliot's Beach for three days. We marched approximately ten miles with full combat gear, spent three days in a fox hole and played war games. It rained while we were out there, so it was a mess when we came back. There was mud on our clothes and boots. Everyone was cleaning their boots and clothes and creating a pile of dirt in the center of the barracks, so I didn´t see anything wrong with cleaning my boots in that pile of dirt too. I was seated down cleaning my boots and the next thing I knew I was lying on the floor. The senior DI had kicked me in the back with his foot, flipping me in the air. I landed flat on my back.

Evidently, we weren't supposed to do that.

We had to be able to run three miles before we could graduate from boot camp. All the times we had run up to this point were in shorts and a short sleeve shirt. This time we had to wear long pants and a long sleeve shirt with the sleeves rolled up, along with boots, a steel helmet, a cartridge belt with magazines, a canteen, and our M-14 in our hands in front of us. I made it but it was rough. The training had helped me push through the challenge, even though I wouldn't admit it.

Richard Perdue, at the end of Marine boot camp

Soon, it was time to graduate from training. Families could come and spend the day with their Marines after graduation, but I knew I wouldn´t have anybody there.

We had a ceremony on the parade deck and every platoon marched at the same time. We had to march, passing in review. Every move was at the same time. Every Marine on the parade deck was exact and precise. It made cold chills run all over you. At that moment, you realized what all the training was for. You had become a unit.

That night we were told where we were going next and what our Military Occupational Specialty (MOS) was. Mine was the 0311 infantry. I was going to Camp Geiger at Base Camp Lejeune in North Carolina. The next morning, we boarded the greyhounds for North Carolina. One could only imagine what it felt like to be leaving Parris Island. We had spent twelve weeks in a place that felt like hell on earth. We didn´t know what the next phase was going to be like, but it felt good leaving Parris Island behind us. They were so hard on us, but it helped prepare us for whatever situation we were placed in. It would all seem like small potatoes compared to boot camp, and if by chance it was worse, we had been made strong from the experience to take it.

I really enjoyed the trip on the buses. We arrived and it was different, but they were still tough on us. Here they gave the people that smoked a break, and they could fall out on the street in formation and smoke. I had never smoked but it didn´t take long until they won me over. If you didn´t smoke, you'd have to stay in the barracks and clean. If those two options were given to most people, I figure most everyone would take the smoking route.

At Camp Lejeune we could go to the post exchange (P.E.) every time we received our paychecks. At Parris Island they took all our money to pay for our clothes and uniforms. Here, I had more time to write Carolyn. I missed her more than I could even explain. We talked a lot about getting married.

They taught us all the basic things about combat. If your MOS was 0311, like mine, you would probably end up in Vietnam. So, we did a lot of jungle training and had a lot of classes. There was also a lot of running and we did a lot of physical training. We got to fire every small arm weapon the Marine Corps had. I guess my favorite one was what they called "The Law." It was a rocket launcher that you fired one time and then destroyed the tube. In an actual combat situation, the tube would be broken up and then buried to prevent the enemy from using it.

Carolyn and I kept talking a lot about getting married when I came home for leave. I would get 30 days leave after Infantry training. Carolyn was 15 and I was 19 but we wanted to get married. Her mother told her she didn´t care if she were to get married but she wouldn´t sign for her. Her Daddy felt more strongly. He offered to set her up in a beauty shop and buy her a new car if she wouldn´t marry me. She wouldn´t go for it.

They took us to a night fire demonstration to show full Marine Corps fire power. It was unbelievable. I could feel the force of the artillery shots make the air bend. By now, we felt like we were the meanest and the baddest people on the face of earth. We felt like we could take the whole world with our bare hands.

Towards the end of November, we received our first leave. On the last day before leave, we went to morning chow and, as had become normal, the three of us then went behind the barracks for a cigarette. We were standing there smoking and none other than our platoon commander walked around the corner. We were caught red-handed only a few hours before going on leave. The platoon commander marched us to his office, hitting the front of our legs and shins with a walking stick along the way. It stung like crazy with each thwack but he didn't let up.

When we arrived at his office, he had us stand at attention in front of his desk as he grabbed a pot of coffee and sat down. He set three coffee cups on top of his desk and poured each one half full of coffee. He then asked us "Does any-body have any cigarettes?" Like a fool I said, "I got a full pack of Marlboro's." He took the cigarettes and poured the tobacco into the cups of coffee. He then took a plug of apple chewing tobacco out of his desk drawer and using his pock-etknife, cut a piece for each cup. By this time, I had figured out where this was going and was dreading what was coming next.

He took a sharpened pencil and stirred the cups up for us all polite-like. Then the order came, "Drink up."

Now I knew we were breaking rules but even before I had picked up the cup I knew it was gonna taste awful, but I was also stubborn. More stubborn than anyone I had ever met. Don't call it a virtue, it's just a fact. While the other two gagged and sputtered as they attempted to keep it down, I gritted my teeth and started throwing it down my gullet. The bitter taste of the coffee mixed with the tobacco tasted like I was eating a newspaper I had found in a dirty puddle. I drank every drop and acted like I liked it.

It was all I could do to keep it down. It was awful but I didn't want him to think it bothered me. He let us go back to the barracks. We put our dress uniforms on to go home. No matter how stubborn I was drinking that stuff down, my stomach could only take so much, and I could feel it start to roll. It was like my gut had hit its breaking point and wouldn't take a moment more of it. I threw up all over my shirt and continued until it was all over the barracks. I had never been that sick before in my life. Thankfully, I had another clean shirt. I changed, stuffed the dirty one in my seabag, and left the barracks for the bus station that took me back to Virginia.

I left the mess for the platoon commander.

I had a long ride to let my stomach calm down. It was a 14-hour bus ride to Virginia. It was also late that day before I could eat, not that I was ready for food. We stopped at a bus station in the upper part of North Carolina, where I finally ate a cheeseburger and an order of fries.

My dream girl was at home waiting for me when I arrived. She jumped into my arms, and I was the happiest guy alive.

CHAPTER 5:
Marine and Wife

Carolyn and I wasted no time trying to figure out how we could get married. My first cousin and her husband said they would take us to Sparta, North Carolina to be wed, and plans were set for the 8th of December. The pastor's wife was a witness along with my mother. We did not have a lot of money at the time, so I don't recall exchanging rings. We came back that evening as husband and wife though and spent our honeymoon at Mommy's house.

Of course, we only had about three weeks left until I had to report for duty at Camp Lejeune in North Carolina. I had missed beer pretty badly while I was at camp and sought to make up for lost time with the drink-same time after I started drinking, Mommy and Daddy were drinking too. One time I was drunk, and I heard Mommy yell from the bedroom. The first thing I thought of was that Daddy was hurting Mommy. I didn't bother figuring out if that's what was going on before I went after Daddy. I don't know if he was being the bigger man or if all the muscle I had gained in boot camp had him worried, but he threw me off him and picked up the kitchen table and put it between us to keep me from getting to him.

I was thinking like a drunk: dumb and with no awareness of what was going on. I later apologized to him. It felt so stupid and bad, knowing I had done that to him over nothing.

It wasn't long though until the time was gone and I had to leave. I went to Rick Creek and got my bus ticket. It was another 14-hour trip by bus, and I had a certain time I had to be there. I hated to leave my newlywed baby doll. It hurt worse now than when I first went into Boot Camp, but I had to go.

I got to Camp Lejeune and reported for duty. I was in the 1st Battalion, 6th Marines, 2nd Marine Division. It was a lot different than bootcamp or infantry training. We had classes or played war games all day. Then if we didn't have any other duty, we would get liberty call and would be off until formation the next morning. It was a lot more lenient than boot camp.

If you had your wife there you could go home earlier, usually around 4 pm. When I heard that, it started the gears turning in my head. I found out that the military required me to put in an application and receive approval for my wife to live on base. I told Carolyn and she was excited, but it would take a while for the paperwork to be processed and get an answer. There were other ways to fill my time although I didn't always make the best choices.

I would go into town on liberty call a lot, and usually that meant I would go out drinking. I started drinking even more after I joined the Marine Corps.

One night I went into Jacksonville and got drunk. I came back to base that night on the bus. Once I stepped off at the bus stop, I started walking towards what I thought was my barracks. All the barracks had a number on them. That's the only way to find the correct barracks because they all looked the same. A jeep pulled up that had two military police, or MPs inside. They asked me where I was going. I told them I was in the 1st battalion, 6th Marines. They said I was going the wrong way and proceeded to tell me where to go. I walked what seemed like forever and in that special drunken way I concluded they had told me the wrong way to go, so I turned around and went the way I was going before. The same MPs came by again and told me to get in the back of the jeep and they'll take me to the 6th Marines. They were gracious guys doing that for me. And so, I finally got back to the barracks.

About every other weekend I would go to Virginia to see Carolyn. When liberty call sounded at 4 pm on Friday I would start my journey. I discovered I could hitchhike in about 6 to 7 hours, compared to the 14 hours by bus.

The young girls would pick you up just to talk. It wasn't hard to tell that you were a Marine when you were standing by the side of the road with your hair cut short and your thumb stuck up. I had to be back on

Richard and Carolyn, after married, parents' house(1969)

base by formation on Monday morning, usually at 7:30 am. I would get home about 11 pm on Friday night and have to leave to go back on Sunday morning.

One time the bus station man told me I could wait until Sunday evening and leave and get there before morning, so I tried it. They were wrong. When I woke up in the morning on the bus and saw where we were I realized I wasn't going to make it. When we pulled off at a bus stop, I went in and called the base and explained what had happened. Thankfully no one ever reprimanded me for my tardiness, even when I was two hours late. Very different from boot camp.

Then one day they told me that I had been approved for base housing. I called Carolyn and she was so happy. I was assigned a trailer to live in. She asked her sister's husband to bring her down there. It was small, about like a camper but we made it work just fine. It was fully furnished so all we needed was food and cleaning materials. Conveniently, we had a small store, called a post exchange (PX), about 100 feet from the trailer. I purchased some food to eat, and I also bought two cases of beer storing them in the closet.

It's a big change for a young girl to start housekeeping on a Marine base with thousands of soldiers. I didn't think about it too much, there were a lot of Marines who had their wives there. She fit in just fine with them, but every once in a while, I would remember that what she was used to and what I was used to were very different.

One day on a weekend I got drunk and started wondering about the big bay of water behind our trailer. I wanted to wade out in the bay to see how deep it was. Carolyn didn't want me to go, but drunk people will do what they do. I went out there and started wading in while she just stood on the bank. I went about 200 yards out, the water never getting over knee deep. When I came back, she was crying and scared to death over what I had done.

Another time we went to the main PX. We had to get a taxi to go there and the driver we wound up with only had one arm. That didn't slow him down though and he took us there flying and cutting in and out of the traffic. She was practically shaking when we got out, and she never went to that PX again.

Still, it was mostly good. On top of having a store real close, there was a bus stop right at the trailer park. So, when we decided to have a baby while

Uncle Sam would pay the bill, we could take the bus to go to the hospital for her checkups.

We really enjoyed our time together there.

Around the first of May I got west pack orders. That usually meant you were going to Vietnam. It also meant Carolyn couldn't live on the base anymore. I would have 30 days of leave and then report to Camp Pendleton, California where I would go through staging before going to the Orient.

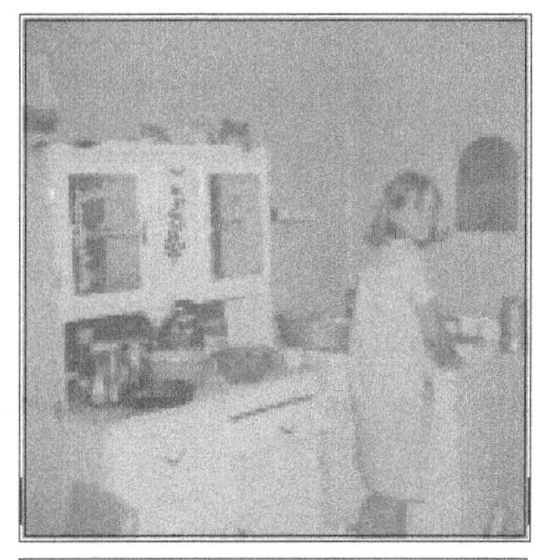

Carolyn at my Mom and Dad's house(1969)

Mommy and Daddy came down and brought us back to Virginia. We had 30 days to spend together and then I would be gone for a year. At the time we didn't know if I would ever be back; a lot of Marines who went to Vietnam only came back in a wood box.

We tried to spend every minute together: Carolyn, me and my family. One day I went fishing with Daddy. They told us at Lejeune that we could fish in any open stream in the United States without a license.

I had just opened a beer and sat it on a rock when I saw something glitter in the sunlight behind me. I turned around and it was the game warden. He said he had to check my fishing license, and I told him what they told me at Camp Lejeune.

He said I should go to the clerk and pay the fine. I went to the courthouse to pay the fine, and once again told them what I knew from Camp Lejeune. Still had to pay the cashier $22. I even had to borrow money from my uncle to pay the fine and mail it back to him. It was okay to go to Vietnam and die for your country, but you couldn't let a fine slide.

We really enjoyed our brief time together, but the day finally came for me to go.

I had to have someone take me to Bluefield to the airport. Daddy didn't want to go and see me leave, but he finally agreed to take me. He said he would take me to the airport and let me out, but he would not stay to watch my plane take off.

We got to the airport, and it was time to say goodbye. I got out and told Daddy goodbye and then hugged Mommy. I got Carolyn in my arms, and I kissed her and kissed her, more and more. If someone has never been in that situation, they have no idea what it feels like. But finally, I had to go so I got my sea bag, turned, and started walking towards the airport. Tears were running down both cheeks. I never looked back because I knew if I did, I wouldn't be able to bring myself to go. When we lifted off the ground I looked, and Daddy's truck was gone. Carolyn told me once that he left as soon as I walked away.

It amazed me looking at West Virginia from the air and seeing how the strip mining had torn up the whole place even back then. I know they didn't stop just because I got a glimpse of it. When we landed at Charleston, I called Carolyn and told her where I was. I was crying so much I could hardly talk. We flew out of Charleston, and over the Great Lakes on our descent into Chicago. There, we had a four-hour layover. I found my way to the bar and drank until it was time to leave. The time came and we left Chicago on our way to San Diego. I got a good look at the farmlands that swept through the Midwest. We also went over the Grand Canyon. Even at 42,000 feet it was still huge.

It was a six-hour flight and then we finally landed in San Diego. There were several other Marines on my flight, so we took a bus to Camp Pendleton and checked in. We didn't want to be late. They showed us where to go to our barracks. We were all 0311. Every Marine knew that if their MOS was 0311, they were going to be sent to Vietnam. We all knew it was a matter of time. We were all stuck in the nasty California desert in July with nothing to look at but the cacti.

The next morning, we fell out for morning formation. They told us what we were going to be doing the next 30 days for training. We got almost no free time--we trained all the time, getting us ready for jungle combat. We didn't really get a break until the end of those 30 days when they gave us a night liberty call.

It was a kind of morbid celebration. We were done with training and try-ing not to think about what comes next. Some of the guys went down to Tijuana, Mexico to have a good time. I wasn't looking for trouble, so I chose not to go with them. Instead, me and some of the other guys went to the ocean side.

California has a 21-year-old drinking age law so I wasn't old enough to buy alcohol. It seemed absurd at the time: I was old enough to die for my coun-try, but not to drink.

We solved that problem soon though. Some of the guys that were older bought liquor for us who were under 21. We walked around town and the beach, and drank our liquor. I got pretty drunk and was feeling no pain or anx-iety anymore. In that moment, I decided I wanted to get a tattoo. Almost every Marine has a tattoo, so I chose a Marine Corps Bulldog on my right forearm, and Carolyn on my left one. I went to the bar and ordered a beer. They gave me a drink that I thought was beer, but it was actually a nonalcoholic beer. They were clever, because I didn't notice the difference.

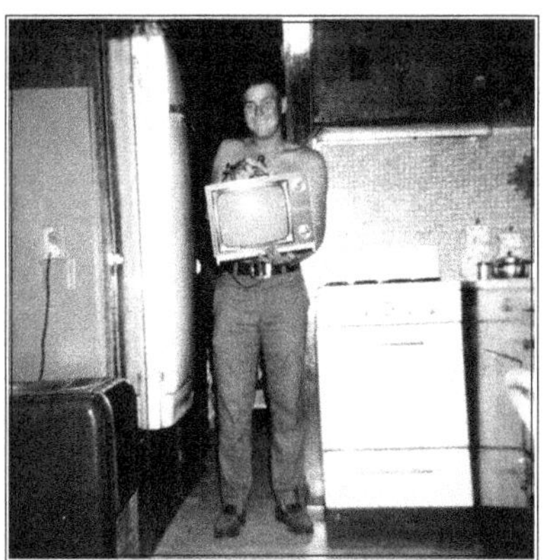

Early years of housekeeping
Marine Corps Base Camp
Lejune, North Carolina

CHAPTER 6:
Separation by Orders

The time came when they told us where our next duty station was going to be. In the Marine Corps, tours were split, spending six months in the Vietnam War and six months in Okinawa, Japan at the U.S. base. When they passed me my orders, I could hardly believe it. Mine said I was going to Okinawa first. I was certain I was heading to Vietnam! At the time I thought it was just a six-month reprieve, but God had his hand on me and was moving the world around in his own way.

Richard-Okinawa, Japan

I couldn't wait to call Carolyn and tell her what the orders were. I explained to her the way it worked in the Marine Corps. I told her that after six months I'd have to go to Vietnam, but I was still excited just to not have to go there now.

We all got on the buses that went to the Air Force base. From there, we loaded onto a DC10--all 283 of us. It was 95 degrees when we left California. We took off and headed north, flying over Seattle, Washington and then over British Columbia. The flight was going to be 17 hours in total to Okinawa. We landed in Anchorage, Alaska about halfway through. We had to refuel so everyone got off the jet for a while. It was about 6 am and 65 degrees. After refueling we headed out over the Pacific. I liked looking down at the scenery but all you could see now was water. At one time I was looking down, and a jet went under us, it must have been a fighter from a carrier. They served us a meal two times while we flew. The way the time zones were changing constantly, it was difficult to keep up with the time. We had flown all night. I hadn't slept for a moment.

At about 6 am the pilot came onto the speaker and said that if you looked to the right, you could see Mt. Fuji. I looked and the snowcapped mountain was jutting out above the clouds. A few minutes later, they cut the engines, and we started our descent to the airport in Tokyo. It was so foggy you couldn't see the wing tips on the jet. Suddenly, the four big jet engines went wide open. The pilot had missed the runway, and the nose of the jet was raised as we started to climb. On the way up we almost hit the tower on the field. We made another pass and landed. We got off the jet, and they refueled.

That was yet another time that God had saved my life, but I was yet to fully fathom His protection.

We got back to the jet, and the next stop was Okinawa. So, a couple hours later, we finally made it to our destination. Some would stay on the jet for Vietnam.

I didn't know who she was, but a blonde stewardess stood at the door and kissed every young man that got off the jet. I thought about it later and that was probably the last kiss some of them ever got. I had to admire that girl.

They picked us up on a six-by-six, which is a tandem truck to take us to our base, Camp Hansen. As we passed through Okinawa I was amazed; I had never seen pictures of a place like this. It seemed familiar but everything about it looked a little different. People looked different. They were short with little ears, slanted eyes, they rode bicycles, and had animals called water buffaloes.

I was assigned to 1st battalion, 2nd Platoon, 4th Marines. They gave me a sack and a locker, and after a day of following everyone else around we all went to bed.

The next morning, we had the morning reveille, the call to get up. We would get up and dress to make sure we could get our breakfast chow. They only served chow at certain times and if you didn't eat at that time, you didn't eat. We ate three meals a day and we burnt all those calories! We had morning formation at 7:30 every morning. A lot of times we would go on a run afterwards. We usually ran six and two-tenths miles. I got to where I was running with the company in the morning and running again in the evening, which was twelve and four-tenths miles a day-not missing a meal was very important.

We were off on Saturday and Sunday unless we had some special

At work in
"the bush", Okinawa

duty such as spending time in the bush, which we were constantly doing. If we were practicing in the trees and dirt there was no time off. When we came back there would usually be several days of cleaning gear and having inspections. We trained all the time and had to always be ready. They could send us anywhere in the world at any time the President decided that we were needed. A lot of times we would have our gear together and stand on the street ready to go and they would cancel.

If you were on barrack duty you would get liberty call at about 4 pm. When we went on liberty call you could stay out all night, but you had better be back at morning formation. You also had better look good because you would not want to be called out by your leaders, and they scrutinized every Marine. I had also always been warned not to volunteer for anything. Sometimes you would be assigned to a work detail wherever they needed something done. Some of the guys had already been to Vietnam and were spending the second part of their tour in Okinawa.

When I first arrived in Okinawa, they had the B-52 bombers stationed there. They would usually leave on a bombing run to Vietnam in the middle of the night. Our barracks were made of concrete but when the B-52s went out they would shake the walls. One time, my unit was being sent to Mt. Fuji for cold weather survival training. They wanted volunteers to stay behind for guard duty. I had always been told to not to volunteer for anything… but I didn't like cold weather, so I volunteered. Guard duty consisted of four hours on and eight hours off. That was the best duty I ever had.

I went on liberty call and explored Kin Ville. That was the town right outside our main gate. The Ville mostly consisted of bars and what they called skivvy houses, or places of prostitution. I walked around one night in the Ville and counted them, 69 in all. The way it worked was the Papa-San, an older

Vietnamese man, would borrow money from the woman who ran the skivvy houses. He would let the Mama-San, or Vietnamese woman, have his daughter for so long to pay the debt depending on how much money he borrowed. Prostitution was legal in Okinawa. A man could go in and look at the girls and decide which one he wanted and pay usually about $5 and then take her to a bedroom.

I am ashamed to admit that a few times I got drunk and took that route. I knew it was wrong, but I was just being stupid. It was something that weighed on my conscience for a long time, until I finally worked up the nerve to tell Carolyn. I lied to her for years. At the end though, Carolyn forgave me. That was all that mattered. Her absolution let me forgive myself and let me know God had done the same.

A person does a lot of things in their lifetime, a lot of which they may regret. In those moments, forgiveness is a beautiful thing, and that beauty is something Jesus Christ has done for fools like me for a long time.

I thought about Carolyn and our unborn baby a lot while I was there. I missed her so much I could hardly stand it. I would look up in the air and watch the commercial airlines go over to try and take my mind off it. Something about the planes slowly moving across the sky would match my mood when I would get like that.

I called Carolyn one night. You had to call and reverse the charges. There was no such thing as a cell phone. We talked for about 30 minutes. She only got $100.00 a month allotment, and it took about all that month's allotment to pay for that call. I always wrote Carolyn every day unless I was in the bush. Writing was a whole lot cheaper than calling and we needed to keep talking. It was getting close to time for our baby to be born.

On December 13th, 1970, I was in the bathroom, and a messenger came and told me I had a phone call from the Red Cross at battalion headquarters. We didn't have a phone in the barracks.

The red cross guy told me our baby was born on December 10th, three days prior, and she was healthy with both mother and child doing fine. I was dumbfounded. I couldn't believe it took three days to get a hold of me. It's not like they didn't know where I was, but it didn't matter. I had a daughter and that was beautiful.

They had us do all sorts of things while we were at the base. One time we got called out to go on riot control to protect the air base. Earlier that year, there had been an incident with some of the locals rioting over us being there. We weren't supposed to actually do anything. We weren't allowed to; just be there as a show of force. Uncle Sam wanted to keep the peace around where His boys were stationed, I suppose.

Another time we had to go to the army base to provide protection. Army and Marine soldiers have a kind of schoolhouse rivalry with each other, so when the two got together it's not always smooth sailing. One day we were marching down the street going to chow. Some of the army guys were outside their barracks laughing at us. When we were marching every movement was precise. Our company gunnery sergeant gave us a command PLATOON HALT and a RIGHT FACE. All the army guys disappeared. We weren't allowed to laugh at that, but seeing them scamper was funny.

When we were finally off the clock, we could be a pretty rowdy group too. There was a guy in another platoon in my company that was different than everyone else. He left an impression on me that has lasted a lifetime. He didn't participate in all the junk the rest of us did. I never got to know him too well, but he had to be a Christian. I could tell the difference even then.

In January, some of the guys in the office came to me and asked if I wanted to go to Vietnam. I asked back "what do you mean?" They had started to pull troops out of Vietnam. I started thinking, Julie is only one month old, I'll get out of the Marine corps in six months. I told them if it's all the same I would stay here; it's not worth the risk. If my orders had said to go, I wouldn't have hesitated.

No orders came and it was a decision I am so happy I made. God had given

C-130 Cargo Plane, Phillipines

me plenty and I just had to call Carolyn and tell her the news that I wasn't going anywhere. She was so happy.

Still, I had to travel even if I wasn't going to war. We were air lifted to the Philippines for jungle survival training on some C-130s. We arrived at Cubi Point where we were assigned a Philippine guide and instructed to go into the jungle with nothing but our clothes on our backs. He was an interesting fella. I could tell quickly that he had earned his title of survival guide from the U.S. military for a reason. He was sharp. He fixed us some rice to eat, which wasn't much for each of us, but it was delicious. He also had a handmade knife for sale. It wasn't anything fancy, but I would have loved to have bought it. Unfortunately, I didn't have the money to buy it.

Richard and a comrade take a break (Okinawa)

After we ate, he told us we needed to build a shelter. He showed us how and then we tried. It seemed like we were making it well, but when the night came and the rain came with it, we were humbled. The Philippine Islands are in monsoon country, and I had never seen it rain so hard in my life. The way we made our shelter was not up to par as it was raining as hard in the shelter as it was outside! We were soaked. It rained all night, and I didn't sleep for a minute.

When in the jungle, pitch black and pouring down rain, my senses were extra alert to everything. Through the rain, there were things that sounded like animals walking in the jungle. I didn't know whether they were birds, monkeys, or tigers, but they kept me plenty awake. We survived the night, and the next day they sent trucks to take us back to our barracks. We felt like we were about to starve. It takes a lot of food to feed a company of Marines that haven't eaten in 24 hours! We went to chow that evening and ate like hogs.

They put us on mike boats-a big, flat bottom boat used to transport gear or troops-and let us off close to a village. We spent the night there. There was a big marijuana patch there so they placed guards so no one would be tempted. The next day they sent trucks to pick us up earlier than expected. There was a typhoon off the coast heading towards us. We were supposed to do some more things, but they cancelled all that and sent us to our barracks.

That night we got paid and received liberty call. Some groups of guys went off base, but I didn't. Instead, we went to a bar on base that had a band. I drank myself until I saw double, something I had only ever done in my life that one time. I had told Carolyn around this time that I had quit drinking in my letters. I hadn't told her I was doing anything like this. We got back to the barracks at about 1 am, and we were flying out the next day at 6 am. Still drunk: I fell and hit my head on a footlocker.

On liberty call, two weeks before going hone

After eating we went to the airport. We didn't have enough planes to take everyone, so I had to stay there at the airport and wait for the C-130's to fly to Okinawa, unload and come back. I waited on the hot asphalt, sobering up. It was a miserable wait that lasted all day. We flew out that night about 11:00 pm. Somewhere out over the pacific I fell asleep. I woke up and the plane was dropping straight down. It about scared me to death. I thought we were going to crash. We had just hit an air pocket. We finally landed in Okinawa.

Phillipines-Hospital Ship "Hope" in background

It was up in the morning and I still had to show up for formation. We went to bush on the northern end of the island and flew up there on helicopters. While on a night patrol walking along a ridge top, we had to be aware of wild boars in that part of the island. Many people don't know, but a wild boar is a dangerous animal if angry-it can knock a grown man off his feet.

I remember that night in our patrolling column there was a black guy at the back. Someone on the front dropped out and got in the weeds, sat down on his knees so no one could see him and as the black guy passed by, he crawled out snorting like a hog. The black guy took off and passed everyone up. We laughed and laughed.

It wasn't all fun and games though. I got word that the corporal who had gone in my place to Vietnam when I had been asked, stepped on a booby trap and lost both legs. I couldn't imagine what that must have been like.

We also got word that there were a lot of protests and demonstrations back in the States over the War-people who did not agree with the military's involvement.

CHAPTER 7:
Homebound

It was getting into the spring and when a Marine only had 100 days to go, they were called a short-timer. We put a three-month paper calendar up on our lockers, and every morning we would mark a day off. All I could think about was going home. I could hardly stand it and was ready to go. I had been gone almost a year, and although Carolyn had sent me pictures of her, I had never seen Julie. She would be about seven months old by the time I finally got to see her.

When they set up flight dates, if they needed extra people to fill up the plane, you might get an early out. My day finally came, and it was two weeks early. I decided I wasn't going to write Carolyn and would sneak in and surprise her. They took me to the airport, and I was to fly out at 2300 hours or 11 pm. I had watched the freedom flights for the last year. Every time I saw one go over, I knew they were going back to the States. I anticipated looking down and seeing where I had stayed for the past several months.

We got loaded on the plane and the pilot came on the PA system, welcoming us to the flight. He said we were loaded to the max and we would be using up all the runway to get up. "Sit back and enjoy the flight," he said. I looked for my base as we climbed into the air, and saw it disappear thousands of feet below me, then laid my seat back and went to sleep. I woke up eight hours later, and we were one hour out of Honolulu, Hawaii. They were serving breakfast, but I didn't eat anything; I was too excited to head towards home.

Going into Hawaii I thought the terrain from the air looked sort of like southwest Virginia. We landed and went into the airport while they refueled. We were going to land in Los Angeles when our flight ended. We would have to go through customs, expecting to arrive on the 4th of July weekend. They picked us up on buses to Camp Pendleton's discharge center. We were then told that this was a holiday week, and we wouldn't be processed until Tuesday. My surprise plans weren't working very well. We had to lay around there all weekend with nothing to do. Tuesday finally came though, and we were processed and paid. We were always paid in cash.

Several of us went together and got taxi cabs to the San Diego airport. I went up to the counter and told them I wanted a ticket for a flight the closest to Roanoke and the fastest I could get there. I got a flight to Raleigh, North Carolina, with a four-hour layover in Chicago. But this time I didn't go to the bar and kill four hours. I went up on the breezeway and watched the jets take off and land.

Finally, my flight started boarding. I was ready to go. We landed at Raleigh airport, where I got off and retrieved my sea bag. I walked into the airport and went to the telephone to call the bus station and see when I could get a bus to Winston-Salem.

The guy behind the counter asked me where I was going. I told him I needed to get a bus to Bluefield, West Virginia. He said the jet I just got off was going to Greensboro, which was closer. He offered to check if I could get back on the plane. They called the pilot and held the flight and I then flew to Greensboro.

I was so close to home yet there was still another leg of the trip to figure out. Three of us chipped in and got a limousine to Winston-Salem. As I got out of the limousine there was a bus backing out that had the sign "Bluefield" on the front. I took off running and beat on the door of the bus, but the driver wouldn't open the door. I went inside and asked when the next bus would be leaving for Bluefield, and he told me it was in four hours. No choice but to wait. I also asked where to get something to eat, and he told me about a place that was four blocks away.

I couldn't stand it anymore; I had to call Carolyn. When she picked up the phone line, I told her I was in Winston-Salem waiting four more hours for the next bus. She said she figured I was on my way home when the letters stopped coming. I asked her if she might ask my Daddy to bring them to Bluefield and get me. It was going to be about 8 am by the time I would get there. She said, "We'll be there."

So, I started on my journey to find some food. I had my dress uniform on, and as I walked down the street, two women came up from behind me and got me by both arms. They said, "we'll just take you home with us." I rejected their offer and told them I haven't seen my wife in a year and that I had a seven-month-old baby girl waiting for me. I was on my way home and nothing was going to stop me. I found the restaurant and got a cheeseburger, fries and a coke. With my hunger satisfied, I went back to wait on my bus.

When I finally boarded my bus for home, it seemed to take forever to travel from Winston-Salem to Bluefield. Pulling into the station though, I looked out the window and saw the prettiest girl on the face of this earth. There was nothing better than coming home after being gone for a year, and had never been that excited in my life. When I got off the bus she ran and jumped into my arms. We kissed and held each other tight, knowing that our forever together had come. Finally, she turned me loose so I could hug Mommy.

Driving home to Narrows, Carolyn was happy to sit on my lap. She had already rented us an apartment at $100 a month. Heating oil was 18 cents a gallon and gas was 30 cents a gallon. It was hard to make it, but we survived. I had to work every hour of overtime I could get. When you do not have any money, everything seems expensive. Looking at how much utilities and gas cost now, those prices were cheap in comparison.

Daddy took us to see Carolyn's mother. She had my baby girl, Julie, and I could hardly wait to see her. Carolyn went in and got her, and when she brought her out, I reached out my hands. My little girl reached out her hands too and came to me just like she had known me forever.

Holding my little girl, Julie

Then we drove to our new apartment, the place we would first live as husband, wife, and the child we could raise together. Carolyn had done a good job; she had already bought groceries and had the electricity and water turned on. We were ready to start housekeeping. I had a little money left from when I got discharged in California, but it wasn't a lot. We were happy just to be together.

CHAPTER 8:
God's Lighted Path

I was on top of the house one day installing an antenna and two women hollered and invited us to church. Carolyn and I had talked before about attending services. I told her that if I ever did go to church, I didn't want to go to one of those where they shouted and hollered. That idea of causing that big of a scene never made sense to me back then. Those two women were from the Pentecostal church. I told them we might come there sometime. Carolyn wanted to go so the next Sunday night we went.

When the altar call was given, she went and was saved. That night I didn't go with her, but seeing how good she felt about it after made me start thinking. The next Sunday we went again and that night when the altar call was given, I went. That was the night I gave my life to Jesus Christ.

During my life, I hadn't wanted to cause anyone heartache but sometimes fell short of my intentions. I also hadn't been able to see the guidance that God had been giving me to help me at those times. I learned you don't have to try to get revenge or make the world pay you back. If you were patient, God would always come through. Maybe not in the way you think, but He always will get the glory. Carolyn and I got interested in being filled with the Holy Ghost. We would stay at the altar some nights till 11 or 12 pm. It is always a good service when you have people seeking the Holy Spirit.

Someone told us one night that if you wanted to hear a good preacher you needed to go to Pearisburg on Main Street, where they had just started a new Pentecostal church. The Narrows congregation had sent members up there to start the church. We just had to go. They had service on Thursday nights, so the next Thursday we went. When we arrived, we just loved the pastor, his wife, and the members. We didn't know at the time, but they were driving all the way from Athens, West Virginia three to four times a week while working full-time jobs. We went to revival in Staffordsville as well. Carolyn received the Holy Spirit that week.

We started feeling like God was wanting us at this new church. We talked to the pastor and told him what we were feeling and that we had just been baptized a few weeks before. The pastor told me that he felt like they had enough people starting the new church, but we convinced him that we felt like this was God's Will. So, we moved our membership to Pearisburg.

About two weeks later, on a Sunday night, I was filled with the Holy Ghost. My body filled with an energy that is indescribable. Sometimes people will speak in a different language, or what is called "speaking in tongues", while others might dance and move their body in excitement. It is an experience like nothing else on earth.

VW Church bus at the church I pastored

We really enjoyed going to Faith Temple Pentecostal Church, started talking to kids we knew, and then bringing kids to Sunday School. One Sunday morning we pulled into church with twelve kids in our Camaro. The pastor couldn't believe it. He even said they should get me a van. And so, it wasn't long until he got a good buy on a green Volkswagen van. After that, I drove the van to church filled with children.

The Church bought some land on Route 460 and started talking about building a church. I had told the pastor that I was a heavy equipment operator. So, he asked me if I thought maybe the company I worked for could do the grade work for the church. I said I would be glad to ask.

I asked the owner and was told I could use whatever I needed. He would take my wages off and just charge for the equipment. It wasn't long before I loaded a 955-K track Caterpillar on the lowboy trailer and headed to Pearisburg. We had to grade a big hill off to level the land out for the church and the parking lot. He wanted to get the grade work done before school was out. He was a school principal, and he would be out all summer. I worked all day at my regular job and then pushed dirt until dark. We also sold a lot of topsoil that helped pay for the loader.

Once I had all the grade work done, I brought a backhoe to dig the footers, and my father-in-law helped the pastor lay the footers off. Once the footers were dug, we got the concrete poured before school was out. The pastor had two teenage boys who came down and stayed in a member's basement. They were good workers and well-disciplined. Their father had taught them well

The church got a loan plus there were a lot of donations coming in. By August, we had the church under roof. We started having services in the sanctuary with just the framing, and had the church built before cold weather. So now we could concentrate on building up the church members. Soon, we were running two Volkswagen buses. They had elected me as Sunday School superintendent, and I was also elected to the Board, selected as a trustee and in charge of visitation. I mowed the grass and cleaned the church. I was busy, all while working a full-time job on construction. I would go visiting with the pastor on Sundays between services. Then two deacons and I would go to the church one night of the week to pray and go visiting.

It was hard to believe at the beginning of the year that this is where my life would lead, but the Lord takes us where we are needed if we listen.

Around that time, Carolyn decided she wanted to apply to become a foster parent. You had no idea who it would be or what kind of shape the child would be in. I told her I didn't mind trying, so she put her application in.

One Sunday night, the foster agency called and said they had a 2-year-old little boy named "Jack", and he was in a mess. Carolyn told them to bring him over. The agency was right; he was a mess. His mother had been running around drinking all weekend and they had taken the little boy away from her. He was dirty and his diaper

"Jack", a child we fostered

was soiled. Carolyn cleaned him and gave him a bottle. Julie was about 7 years old, so he fit right in with our family. We took him to church, and he would sit in the chair with us, raise his little hand high and holler "praise the Lord." We brought him to see his grandmother who was better put together. Unfortunately, sometime after that his grandmother's husband shot and killed her and then killed himself. Thankfully, Jack was not there to see it.

I was still working my day job when I wasn't building up the church. One day I was working for a local production plant using our equipment to do all their repair work. I was digging a hole for them, working in the acetone recovery area, with three laborers from the company with me. It was in the wintertime, and it was cold. There was a small booth beside where I was digging. It had a telephone and a heater in it. We had been going in there off and on all day to get warm. Suddenly, I heard a rumble and then an explosion. The explosion knocked the three men with me into the hole I was digging.

We had no idea what was happening. I looked up on the roof of the building where there were large six-foot vapor lines. They looked like a big hand had crushed them. I jumped off the backhoe and there was a big piece of metal, about three-by-six feet that had flung into the other side of the backhoe I had been working on. Three units had exploded, and the metal had been thrown everywhere. You could look at the booth and see that the explosion had blown from the inside to the outside.

The safety superintendent pulled up to see if we were alright. He said we should go to the medical center to get checked out and take something to calm down. I told him I didn't need anything to calm down, but he insisted, if I wanted to keep my job I needed to take it. It took contractors six months to build it back. God was still on the throne; He had work for me still left to do.

Construction back then had a way of being quite dangerous. Another time I had to stop at Appalachian Power in Glen Lyn to do a job. Greggory Trucks had brought the excavator to me from another job. To lower the lowboy trailer, the operator had to manually drop it and the only good place to do it was by the three main line railroad tracks beside the power plant. The driver told me to get across the tracks and watch the trailer. If it looks like it is going to get snagged or fall, I had to wave my arms. I told him I didn't believe it would work. He said he'd hit it hard and it could slide on the rails, but when he let it out and I saw it coming off the trailer, I knew it wasn't going to make it.

About the time that the lowboy covered all three tracks on the main line, it hung. The driver tried to pull out, but when he let the clutch out on the tractor it just jumped up and down. It was snagged and covering all three of the railroads. I was terrified at the thought that a train loaded with coal might come down the mountain, around the curve and hit that truck and excavator, knocking it into that giant substation that we were parked next to.

I took off running as hard as I could into the Appalachian Electric Power company building, to the first office I found, and yelled to call N&W railways and tell them to stop all the trains. I was panicked; anyone could see so they didn't ask questions and just did it.

When I got back out there, there was already a N&W man in a truck pulling up. I asked him how long we had until a train would pass by. He said "If you had been one minute later with that phone call you wouldn't be asking that."

We had just barely saved our skin and the lives in that oncoming train. We took a 988 Caterpillar loader and put the bucket under the lowboy and excavator and then carried it across the tracks. I couldn't imagine the amount of money it would have cost if that substation had been hit by our doing, and I was sure thankful I never had to find out.

Faith Temple Church bus, in the Christmas Parade

Julie and I with church bus

CHAPTER 9:
Finding Joy After Sorrow

My father-in-law, Shine got to where he wasn't feeling good. All he looked forward to was retiring, and he was about 62 years old, so the time was approaching. His stomach had been hurting a lot, so he went to a doctor in Narrows who told him he had ulcers. He took about a month off from work but wasn't getting any better.

Shine then decided to see another doctor, in Roanoke this time. The medical staff ran tests on him, although they didn't have the technology that they do now. They found out that he had cancer, but they couldn't find out where it was located in his body.

Carolyn and I went down there a lot and stayed with him. I was sitting there in the room one day and he asked me how many people were in the room. I told him there were three of us. He responded, "there are four. No matter how many are in here, there is always one more," he said.

One Sunday, Shine was back at the hospital, and the pastor came to see him. He told me after we left the hospital that Shine had told him what he had offered Carolyn not to marry me. Probably at that time he was right to do so. I was still young and hadn't found any purpose in life beside Carolyn.

Shine had also said "I could have searched the world, and I couldn't have found her a better husband." That meant a lot to me coming from him. Even today, that still means so much coming from someone I respect like Shine.

We went back home and later that night they had to take him back to the hospital again. The next night I was going to stay with him, but his boy Bob said he'd stay with him.

I was in Stoney Creek the following morning, making a horse riding track for a client. It was after lunch when they came to tell me Shine had passed away. It hurt me deeply. We had worked together every day for the last seven years.

Shine's brother, Prince, and our pastor preached the funeral. The pastor and his wife sang "I'll See You in the Rapture." I thought to myself that this construction company would never survive without Shine, but somehow life went on.

Carolyn was obviously distraught after Shine's passing. She had difficulty coping with her Dad's death and dealing with daily activities for a while. During that time, she decided she couldn't take care of Jack anymore, so she called social services and told them he would need a new home. We later found out that his mother's brother who lived in Charlotte, North Carolina, and was an engineer for Celanese, adopted him. It was good to know he still had family to look out for him even if we couldn't.

Shine had loaned me his truck, but now that he was gone, I needed a new truck. So, I bought a new 1977 Ford pickup. That was the first truck I had ever owned.

At this time, I started feeling like the Lord was calling me to preach. Carolyn said she was feeling the same way. I spoke several times at the church where we got saved and told the pastor what I was feeling. He didn't want me to leave but I felt like I needed to.

I taught a young adult Sunday school class and preached a lot of the time on Sunday nights. The pastor and I were taking a lot of classes from Emmanuel College, the Pentecostal College in Georgia. Our classes were held in Dublin and Bluewell, West Virginia.

Julie was now seven years old, and we felt like we wanted to have another child, so, we tried and soon Carolyn was pregnant.

CHAPTER 10:
Troubled Times, An Ever-Present Savior

A new challenge had surfaced. The house where we lived had a big rock wall beside it and with all the recent rain, that rock wall fell. Some of the rocks were big and Daddy told me that when I got ready to move the rocks to let him know, he would help me.

I thought I was a big tough Marine, and I needed no help. I didn't have to pick the rocks up; I could just have rolled them to where I was going to move them. I reckon I had something to prove to myself. I picked them up and put them in the wheelbarrow to get rid of them.

The next morning, I got up and went to the sink to wash my face. When I bent over, the small of my back stung like an angry hornet. I did what any man does when he makes a dumb decision and ends up in a whole lot of pain from it: I pretended nothing was wrong and ignored it.

At that time, Carolyn decided she wanted to go work at the sewing factory. She went for an interview and got a job pressing shirts. I bought her a car so she could travel by herself. So, then I had two vehicle payments. She also started to constantly feel unwell. It was every day or two I would have to take her to the doctor or the emergency room. I had two different doctors tell me that I ought to divorce her. That was downright frustrating to hear. I told them that those marriage vows we took didn't say you stay with them until they got sick and then ditch them on the curb like the week's garbage. It said until the day you die, and I had no interest in entertaining an alternative.

I kept trying to work, but the pain in my back was getting worse and Carolyn had quit working. With two vehicle payments and a house payment on one income, I didn't know what was ahead of me, but I had faith that God would take care of it.

Since I was taking Carolyn to see the doctor so often, one day I decided to tell him about my back. The doctor recognized a potential problem faster than me. He said he could send me to the hospital where they have two good back doctors.

I went to see one of them and he put me in the hospital for seven days in traction. They hooked ropes to you with weights on them which put a constant pull on your back in an effort to get it sorted. It was constant traction work, and the nurses couldn't keep up with everything else they were doing and at times I would have to holler at them to move me or take me out of the traction.

MRIs didn't exist in 1977 to check a person's back, so instead they had a whole other evaluation process. It was called a myelogram. They'd put the patient on a table that would tilt. Next, they would tap into the person's spine like a pine tree and remove fluid to check you for cancer. They also injected dye into your spine and watched it with x-ray equipment. The whole time the patient is numbed up, but it didn't feel like it. Apparently, they can't numb nerves in bones or something like that, because it was mighty painful. Then once they had the dye in your spine, they tilted the bed down at the head so the dye would travel through your spine. They were watching all this on a screen. The test results showed that I had a swollen disc in my lower back.

After a myelogram, the patient must continue to lay flat on their back for 24 hours. I was told if I raised my head off the bed, the medical staff would have to give me a shot to knock me out. I had to use a urinal too. I'm sure glad my bowels didn't move. I don't know how that would have worked.

When I ate, I had to do it with my head lying flat on the bed. An incredibly awkward experience. I was in the hospital for seven days by myself. Carolyn said she didn't feel like coming over there. Not sure why, but could have been her health problems, or the fact that she was pregnant and the idea of driving in that state is not desirable. The nurse didn't think highly of that though.

She told me when she brought my food in that it would be nice if I had someone there to feed me. Of course, she never offered to do so; she just sat the tray on the bed. I would have to reach for the food on the tray and made a mess doing so.

The next day they told me that the doctor was going to put an injection of Cortisone in the disc that was swollen. The procedure was done in my hospital room. First, he gave me a shot to numb the area, and then he stuck the needle into the disc in my back. It hurt so bad I could hardly keep from screaming out at him. They kept me there one more day and then finally let me go home.

I had to go back and see Dr. Estrella about every two weeks, but the pain was apparently worth it; he said I was getting better. There were times the pain would hit me, and it was unbearable.

Being sick is very expensive, and I knew I was going to have to do something about the cost of my vehicles. The bank would have to repossess them if I couldn't pay, and if they took both, we would be in a bad place. I wouldn't be able to go to the doctor or go back to work once I was in good shape again.

I didn't know what to do, so I decided to talk to a close Brother in the Church. He said I needed to take both vehicles over to Christiansburg, pull them up and park them in front of the bank, go in and ask to speak to the bank president. So, I did.

My Church Brother told me to explain the situation to him and that I couldn't make the payments anymore. The bank president said he admired me for what I was doing and that nobody had done that before. He also said "I'm going to take the car and sell it and get what I can get out of it. I want you to keep the truck, and don't worry about the payment for now. When you get through this and go back to work, then you can resume payments on the truck".

I never did get a bill for anything on the car. He must have been able to pay back my whole car loan with the car as it was.

The Faith Temple Church knew we were in a rough spot and took up a love offering for us. That was mighty nice of them and meant a lot. Still, it wasn't enough to keep us afloat. Finally, I decided I had to sell our house if we were going to survive. Carolyn's brother told me I needed to go to social services and sign up for food stamps. I did and it helped too.

When I bought my house, I paid $7000 for it. So, I put an ad in the newspaper for $16,000 and sold our house. We moved to a rented house on Main Street.

Carolyn's mother sold Shine's truck and had planned to sell his Cadillac too. It was a 1970 Coupe Deville with new metallic green paint: like just off a new car lot. I gave her $700 for it. We were able to get by just like that for a while, for which we were thankful.

It was getting up towards Christmas then, and Carolyn had been praying for a Christmas baby. Christmas Eve night came, but still no baby. When we went to bed that night, it was blowing snow outside. Around 1:00 in the morning, she yelled at me and said it was time! So, I got up, and we headed to the Blacksburg hospital.

One little detail worth mentioning. A few weeks before that, we were settling down to sleep. Carolyn asked me to retrieve a pillow for her situated at the foot of the bed. Without thinking, I sat up to get it for her and heard something pop in my back. I had ruptured a disc.

Sitting around in that hospital, trying to be excited about the birth of my next child, was miserable with a ruptured disc in my back.

God always said he would never put more on you than what you can bear. Sitting in that hospital felt like he was trying to show me all I could endure. Thankfully, He helped by giving me some more of His strength to endure long enough, and I was there to welcome my daughter Jamie into the world.

*****

Julie was now eight years old and happy to see her new sister. We were hoping for a boy, but because we waited to find out the sex of the bay, we chose to name whatever baby God gave us Jamie.

We loved Jamie and were just happy to have another child to add to our family. Carolyn was also ecstatic God gave her to us on Christmas, just like she had been praying for.

That night at about 9 pm, Jamie started crying. Carolyn tried to nurse her, but she kept crying. I laid her across my shoulder and started walking around the house. If I was walking, she would quit crying. When I stopped walking, she would start again. I was hurting so badly I could hardly stand it, but I found out that night I could tolerate more than I thought. I was still walking when it became daylight outside.

We called the doctor, and he said Carolyn might not be producing enough milk to satisfy Jamie. He told us to get some formula and see if it would help. So, I bought some baby formula, and we fixed her a bottle; she ate like she was starving. Carolyn burped her and she went to sleep for the next four hours.

This was all a new experience for me because I was on the other side of the world when Julie was born. Dealing with a newborn was a trial, but through the pain, I loved my time with Jamie at the beginning of her life. Both of my kids were Daddy's girls. God had blessed me and Carolyn with two beautiful children. There was nothing that I wouldn't do for them.

Chapter 11:
A Persistent Problem

I was trying to do the best I could with my back. I went to see Dr. Estrella again, and he released me back to work; however, I knew beyond a shadow of doubt that I wasn't able. I was a mess and only getting worse.

Somebody told me about a Dr. Rob in Bluefield. I called up there and made an appointment. It was on the same day that Carolyn had to go back to see Dr. Smith for her six-week post-natal checkup. Her appointment was in the morning and mine was that evening, so we would be spending the day in the car mostly. I was feeling pretty good when I got up that morning, so I didn't take any pain medication. This is what doctors would call "a mistake".

I started hurting when we got to Pembroke, and the further we went, the worse the pain got. We got to the top of Brushey Mountain and I pulled off the road. I walked around the front of the vehicle, trying to get relief, but there was no way I could move to reduce the pain. With every breath it felt like I was getting stabbed in the back. Again, I wanted to scream through the pain, but that would help nothing and only make things worse.

After taking a painkiller and waiting for it to kick in, I could only get back in the car and drive. Dr. Smith said everything looked good to Carolyn, but he couldn't say the same thing about me. The drive there made me twice as bad compared to even before I left home. I was bent over at the waist like an old man. My hip was pushed to the side, and I was dragging my left foot behind me as I hobbled about. I was not a pretty sight.

We made it back home, but I still had to go to Bluefield to see Dr. Rob. I took another painkiller and started on my journey. It wasn't a good trip. Every bump I hit in the road almost took my breath. Nice thing about roads nowadays is they are paved fairly smooth. This was not true back then and, boy, my back was letting me know it.

I made it to Bluefield, went into the doctor's office, and with just one look at me, they knew I was in a bad way. The nurse took me back for an x-ray. She tried to help me get on the table but her help only made my back flair up worse. I told her to let me do it, and I got myself up there eventually. Thankfully, we made it through the x-rays.

Dr. Rob said he was going to call Duke University and check if they could see me. He said they had a good back surgeon there. The doctor was also a professor at the university, so him calling it in assured the appointment.

Daddy and my brother-in-law, Virgil, agreed to take my truck and drive me down to Duke and then leave me there. My appointment was at 8 am so we had to leave in the middle of the night. I took a pain pill, and we drove the four-hour drive. Upon arrival, we went into the hospital, and they put me in a room to wait for the doctor.

I was sitting there on the bed doing nothing and suddenly the pain hit me. I tried to get up and move my back to make it more tolerable, but nothing. I just had to sit there hurting like there were hot coals in my back. Every minute felt like ten, just waiting for someone to show up and evaluate me.

The doctor finally came in, and she had to check to see if I was bad enough to have surgery. After an extensive exam she decided they would keep me. So, I told Daddy and Virgil they could go home, and we would go from there.

On a Friday, I was checked into a room with two other patients. I asked if I could have a private room. They said there was no such thing as a private room there; "you are lucky enough that you got a bed." I didn't feel lucky, not one bit but they were the professionals so what did I know.

Duke was a teaching hospital and so the next two days I was examined by a lot of different students. At first it wasn't all that bad, but it started becoming a nuisance after a while. The exams tended to just make my pain worse, and *I* wasn't learning anything from the experience.

They scheduled me for surgery on Monday. I had to get up early and take a shower before surgery. Even something that small was an ordeal. By the end of that shower, I felt like I had just completed basic training again. Some accomplishments look a whole lot different when based on your limitations.

They took me to surgery and gave me a shot. In minutes, I didn't have a care in the world. They also gave me a spinal injection and then I couldn't feel anything.

This kind of surgery was an odd feeling. You're awake all the way through the surgery and the anesthesiologist talks to you, but like I said, I didn't have a care in the world as they cut me open. You needed to be that out of it to handle the time I suppose. The surgery lasted about four-and-a-half hours.

By the end of the process, it felt like someone had torn a chunk out of my spine. To deal with the pain, they started putting morphine in my IV every ten minutes. They also told me not to smoke for so many hours after they took me back to the room. I couldn't stand it, and I figured it was probably just a precaution they took. I got a cigarette out and smoked it. It made me horribly sick, and I threw up everywhere. It was not a precaution.

During that time while I was recovering, I learned what it was like to be a drug addict. The pain was terrible, and I would watch the clock just waiting with sweat on my face. When it got time for my next dose, whether I needed it or not, I was hollering for it. The relief it gave helped so much but it was addicting for sure.

I went to sleep from the morphine, and someone woke me up and said my wife was on the phone. I talked to her just a few minutes and told her I was okay and went right back to sleep.

They gave me morphine all that night and then the next day started switching me to weaker pain medicine. They knew what they were doing. I couldn't imagine what it would have felt like going from the morphine to nothing.

I would stay five days in the hospital after surgery and then could go home. After what I had been through, staying in bed for five days felt like a pretty good plan.

Carolyn's brother and Oneda agreed to come to the hospital and bring me home. Spending eight days there, by myself, I was ready to go home.

They put a brace on my back and told me to walk one minute, two times per day.

The doctor told me, "When you leave Duke, stay on a hard mattress, watch how you lift and keep your weight down." I asked him about the heavy equipment I run at my job. He said it would probably be better if I could find another job.

I asked if he was going to give me a prescription for pain medicine, he said "If you think you will need pain medicine, we'll just keep you here." I just said I was fine. I was getting antsy to head home, so we did just that, and went back to Narrows.

CHAPTER 12:
Many New Beginnings

At first, I didn't listen to the doctor and tried to go back to my old job. I learned fast that some things that used to be easy would not be that any longer. Sitting on that heavy equipment all day was murder on my back, and I experienced consistent pain. Every chance I got, I would walk around.

After putting up with the pain for a short time, I filled out an application at a production plant for a pipefitters job. The problem was they were shored up with folks: the only way you could get a job there was to replace someone who retired or quit. I would have to get mighty lucky to get a position.

At that time, I felt like God was wanting me to go back to Pearisburg to Faith Temple. I didn't know why then, but I went. Soon, I understood why God was pulling me in that direction. They needed groundwork done for a parsonage they wanted to build.

I asked the boss, and he said it was okay. Same deal as before, rent the equipment minus the wages. So, I loaded up the Caterpillar track loader and took it to the church.

The only thing I needed to do was to dig water and sewer lines from Route 460 to the house. Using the excavator, I dug approximately 200 yards of ditches in four hours. My boss dropped by after lunch and he was amazed that I had dug that much ditch in that little amount of time.

I had a lot of respect for the pastor. He was an evangelist when I was there before, and he preached a revival for us when we were on Main Street before we built the church. I thought he was the best evangelist I had ever heard. He gave me the job driving one of the buses again. It was the same bus I drove before, just a different route.

One day after that job I got a call. The Plant had an interview for me. I was afraid my boss would see me leave the site and go over there for the interview. He had done me favors with the equipment and the last thing I wanted him thinking was that I was disloyal, especially if I didn't get the job. It just so happened, the day I went for my interview it rained so we didn't work that day.

I passed my interview. I also learned the importance of the college course on blueprint reading I had taken overseas. When they gave me a paper test to fill out, I knew the answers and passed. They scheduled me to take a shop test as well, which I also passed. Then, they sent me to talk to the maintenance superintendent, and he asked if I knew anything about pipefitting. I answered honestly and told him no, but I was willing to learn. That was exactly the words he wanted to hear from me, he said.

I called my boss on construction to tell him I had accepted another job, and I had made arrangements to work out a two-week notice. That would allow me time to teach someone to operate the excavator.

He wasn't thrilled to hear that. He grumbled, "I've got enough problems with the rain." I said I was just trying to be nice about it. He told me not to make any decision until we had a chance to sit down and talk. That talk never took place.

I was going to be working from 3 to 11 pm. Those hours were brutal, but they said there was a man that was going to retire, and I could bid on his job when he leaves. I only made $6.25 an hour in the new position, and I was making $6 per hour on construction, but the benefits were better. The only benefits we had on construction were health insurance.

It was a big change for me. I thought I was going to be doing pipe work all the time. The first job I got was with someone else washing out a vessel with a water blaster. The acid fumes kicked me like a mule's hindlegs. It was a new smell and new type of discomfort to get used to. This was the first time I had ever worked maintenance in an industrial plant too. I didn't like the 3-11 shift; I always hated having to go to work in the evening when the sun was shining bright.

All the people I worked with were a great group of men. They would do anything to help you, but not everyone was perfect. An old man working there told me one day that the best way to make it in a job was to watch everybody do the work and then decide the best way for you to do it. Many people will do the job differently, but accomplish the same results in the end.

There was overtime available, and I worked every shift I could get. With that overtime I started raking in cash like I never had before. For four months, I continued working the night shift before the daylight job came open. I bid on it, and I got to enjoy daytime again.

On dayshift, I went on the project crew and was back to doing stuff I knew like rebuilding equipment and laying pipes. I could still work overtime on maintenance when it was available, and I took it when I could.

Soon, it was my first Christmas there and my foreman asked me if I would go to the radio station and wish all the community a Merry Christmas on behalf of the company. So, I had the opportunity to be on the radio. Some of the men were annoyed I did that and teased me for it. They had the chance to go, and they declined. I wanted to do it, so I chose to ignore their chiding.

Sometimes working at such a big company, I would get the impression that people weren't always happy with me or even aggravated with me. When we were face to face though, they seemed to like me. The way I see it, taking people on the surface value is all I can do. If they don't tell me how they feel, then how can I change? Besides, it's best just to worry about my own flock than to worry about how people may or may not see me.

One of the places I worked at the plant was in the furnace room, a building five stories tall filled with cookers. The furnaces were used to make anhydride- an acidic acid used to turn wood pulp into liquid. Sometimes we had to go into the furnaces to fix things, but the furnaces even when off were hot. The pipes were cherry red. If you were to step on one, it would melt the soles on your boots.

One time my foreman sent me there by myself to perform a task. I hadn't been there long enough to know any better. I went up there and did what I had to do, and when I came down, my feet had only touched the floor for a few seconds before a gasket blew in the furnace and anhydride went everywhere. If I had been there when it happened, I would have been covered in anhydride acid. The other men on our crew chewed the foreman out good for that one.

When we were working and using cutting tools you could barely see the walls, there was just so much dust floating in the air. No one ever told us about the asbestos. After they built new furnaces outside, they roped the whole building off with tape that said, "no admittance, asbestos hazard."

My foreman always expected more out of me than he did for the rest of men. I always figured it was because we went to church together, but it could have just been because of all the overtime I would work. Looking back, I think he saw potential in me and wanted me to learn.

When production was slow, I would be moved to work in another department. When production came back up, the foreman wanted me back on projects. He said, "If you come back to the project crew, I will let you work with whoever you want to". I told him that I liked working on maintenance. It wasn't so hard on my back and had some of the type of work that I enjoyed. He obliged me and let me work just as I wanted.

In September 1980, five months after I started working at the plant, my wife and I started thinking about buying another house. We were looking around and saw little Jack's grandmother's house had a "For Sale" sign in the yard.

I called the number on the sign, and it was the very man who adopted Jack. After Jack's grandmother and grandfather had died in the murder suicide, they were looking to sell the house. I offered him $30,000 for the house and he took it. I applied for a loan with FHA, and they approved it.

A quick side note: it all seemed fine for eight years, but evidently something went wrong. A missed payment or something led them to tell me I needed to get financing from elsewhere. That's when I realized FHA loans pay off interest before the base of the loan. I was fuming when I saw how little of the principal of the loan I had paid off in those years.

When we were moving into the house though, Carolyn started helping her mother. Her mother was babysitting, and she paid Carolyn $10 a day to clean her house. The problem was, Carolyn couldn't keep up with even that. She got to where she was staying so tired she could hardly go.

She finally went to a doctor over in Dublin. They did bloodwork on her and they told her she had Hepatitis. The way you get it is through sex or get stuck with a dirty needle. We knew it wasn't sex because if it was I would have contracted it too.

The only conclusion we could reach was that it must have been at the dentist; just about the only place she was getting stuck with a needle. Back then, instead of using new needles they would sterilize the needle and use it again. Of course, with no evidence, we couldn't do anything about it but get her treated.

After a few months she started to feel better, but she was having problems getting out of the house. She wanted to stay home all the time, although she did take her mommy down to Corner Stone Church one night and she got saved.

When Shine had passed away, he had left Carolyn's mother a good bit of money. They had bought three houses to rent so she would have extra money each month. She sold one to Carolyn's brother, Bob. Jeff moved into one and Jody rented the other one.

Carolyn said to me one day, "I want to give you something to pray about." She said her mother didn't want to go to Corner Stone anymore. She too was getting anxious about leaving the house. "Can you pray about building a church out in the garage?"

I said I'll pray about it. Not only did I pray about it, that one request started me on a long path. I would build a church.

On Carolyn's mother's property, I planned to make a place for her to pray. We would have services on Thursdays, not taking away from the Sunday Corner Stone Church services on Sunday.

We would work to get people saved and then take them to Corner Stone. We would use a different preacher every night. It all started growing and becoming its own incredible thing. I told the pastor at Corner Stone what I was going to do. He said it was okay.

The pastor's boy (I will call him Henry for the sake of confidentiality) was a good friend of mine. He was an ordained minister. He had been a pastor but now was an evangelist. He agreed to help me do the work.

Henry doing that for me made me so grateful, and I felt like I needed to do something nice for him and his wife.

There was a furniture discount store over at Hillsville and it was huge.

So, I told them one day I would like to take them to the store and buy them something. I didn't have any money, but I picked them up anyway and we went to Hillsville's Triangle Furniture. We walked into the store, and I told them to pick out the living room they wanted, and I would pay for it. We got a full living room of furniture. It was all I could do to pile it on my truck. We had to tie the furniture on the truck with ropes to keep it from falling off. I wrote the man a check for almost $1300.

On Monday, I went to the credit union and borrowed money to cover the check I had written and paid payments on it until it was all paid for.

We went to work on building the church. We were working in the evenings and on Saturdays. If I was building a church, I would want to build it right. I put a big air conditioner in, an oil furnace for heat, and built an altar across the front of the space. The sanctuary would seat about forty people. I think it might have costed me a couple weeks' vacation to have enough time to get the work completed.

I asked Henry if he would preach some for me, and he said he would. He also brought his father, the pastor, to look at the church. The pastor said it looked nice, but when he saw the altar, he kind of made a face. The next day, Henry told me that his daddy didn't want him to help me anymore. I told him I would have to make that decision, but he said, "Sorry, I don't want to have bad feelings with my dad." I said that I hated it, but God will work it out.

I asked myself what to do and just started to pray. Someone told me about a preacher over at Ripplemead. I called him and he agreed to come. Of course, that preacher had no interest in taking the people to another church after our services, so the idea of getting them saved and taking them to Corner Stone was gone.

We decided to have service three times per week like any other church, and we named it "Evangelistic Outreach Ministry." Julie had taken piano lessons so I asked her if she could play the piano for me. She said she would try. I called Kyle Dent and asked him if they could come and sing for us and he accepted.

We had our first service, and everything went great. Kyle Dent, Vernice Fleeman and Brother Willey Hedrick could really sing. The biggest problem we had was parking, but we managed it well. Word got out about the services and people were coming.

Brother Townley, Sister Raines from Peterstown, and Sister Jan Pardom were taking turns preaching and I would fill in when we didn't have anyone. We had bought a 15-passenger Dodge van, and it was coming into services filled with churchgoers.

I would also teach Sunday school. The Lord really blessed us, and the place was full just about every service.

After about a year, Carolyn's mother expressed that because she owned the property, she wanted to have a say in the church. She wanted to use Sister Rains instead of all the different preachers. That was not the way it was set up in the beginning, so I decided I was going to get out of the logistics before it got all messy.

I felt God also had called me to make a move elsewhere, and everyone involved was happy with the way I handled things.

On the last Sunday night I was at the ministry we built, I brought the message about the "sin of Ananias and Sapphira." Another church was eventually purchased in Pembroke, and I taught adult Sunday School there for a long time.

Chapter 13:
Long Hours

Carolyn was still having trouble with her nerves. Her mommy had baby-sat for years, but she was getting older, so she decided she was going to quit keeping children. Carolyn seemed like she did better when she had her mind occupied so she started babysitting the kids her mother had.

She was babysitting from home and spent the next seven years house-bound. I had to get the groceries, arrange parent and teacher conferences, or anything else that had to be done outside our home. It was stressful and coping was difficult. I guess my route of escape became my shop.

I built two sections onto my shop, and I bought a lot of equipment. I worked in my shop every day of the week, with work I'd be moving my hands from 4 am to 9 pm normally. I'm sure my family felt neglected at times from my devotion to work.

Sometimes, I would work three days solid in the shop and working over-time at the plant. It would get to the point that some days, I was just a walking zombie.

Carolyn's sister bought four houses, so I remodeled them all from the ground up. Then after she got them rented, I took care of all the maintenance on them.

In 1985, I bought a new Ford XLT truck. It was a pretty thing. One day the windshield started leaking so I called the dealership and got an appointment at the body shop to get it sealed. I had known the foreman of the body shop for years. He had painted a car for me in his own private shop. When he saw me, he told me that the truck had been wrecked and had a new top put on it. I said I would take it down to the showroom to see the salesman and they would take care of it.

When I got to the sales room there was no salesman to be found. So, I went to see the shop foreman, and he told me to get my warranty card, and he would get the paperwork started. Some regular smart aleck walked up behind us and he told the shop foreman that there was no use filling out any warranty on that truck because it was sold "as is" without a warranty. It was supposed to have a sign on the window.

This was when they first passed the law that said that if you sold a vehicle it had to have a sign in the window saying if it had a warranty. Obviously, there was no such sign when I paid the same price as a new one.

I went off on them. I told them to tell the salesman he had better call me as soon as possible. Of course, I never have seen the salesman again. I don't know if he quit or if he was hiding.

The owner of the dealership called me one night and talked to me like a dog. He wanted me to bring the truck over there and let them fix it. I rejected the idea and said that I just bought a new truck and that's what I wanted it to be.

I filled out a complaint with the appeals board of Ford Motor Company. In my complaint, I agreed they could let any garage in the United States fix the truck, but the dealership I purchased it from wasn't going to touch it.

They had a hearing and made their decision that I had to take the truck over to the dealership where I purchased it and let them fix the truck. I wrote them a letter back and told them what I thought of their response. I paid for fixing the truck out of my own pocket.

Chapter 14:
Sorrow and Unease

During this time of my life, I am going to tell a story that really affected my whole family. I'm not going to disclose any names that might dishonor anyone.

Carolyn's mother's health started to go down. She had osteoporosis, she even walked bent over with her head looking down towards the ground. Julie and JJ would take turns bringing meals to her. She lived like this for about two years.

One day JJ took dinner to her and sat the food on the bar. When he was leaving Miss Perdue kind of raised her hand and JJ thought she was thanking him for the food, so he waved at her and went on out the door.

Later that day someone else went over there and she had passed out. There was no response. They took her to the hospital and said she had a stroke. She never recovered and after about three days they unhooked all life support.

They had the funeral at her church in Pembroke. This would be the last service they would have in that church. The family later sold the church and divided the money amongst the kids. Her house had gone down a lot, and it needed many repairs. The family put it up for sale and it sat there for a year. I had been doing all the repairs on it except for the last several years. I just didn't have the time.

I told Carolyn one day that she could talk to her brothers and sisters, and if they wanted me to do the repairs on the house to get it ready to sell, I would. They could pay me after it was sold. I did the repairs and John; my son-in-law helped me. It needed a lot of work.

They put a "For Sale" sign on it, and it sold within 30 days.

My only prayer is that the ones who are left, that one day, somehow, they will humble themselves and call out to Jesus Christ and ask him to come into their hearts and save their soul. I am not interested in revenge.

*****

My wife called me one day at work and said that she had something to tell me, and she said, "You're not going to believe it," which only increased my curiosity. Once I heard what she had to say, she was right; I couldn't believe it. A boy was getting naked in a window, playing with himself in front of my wife, along with a yard full of little kids she was babysitting. Both of my girls were there too: Julie was a senior in high school at the time.

I knew I had to do something but what, I asked myself. This boy had family in the police force, so I knew that route was out, plus everybody in the county feared them. Rumor was, if you make this family mad at you, they will seek revenge. Everyone was afraid… except one crazy marine.

There is a saying, *you don't want to fight if you don't have to; back up as far as you can go.* However, there is also the saying, *if you back on an old dog in the corner and there's no way out, he will bite you.*

I knew I didn't have the answer to this little problem, so I prayed. One of the women Carolyn babysat for worked for social services. I talked to her, and she said that if I confronted their parents you need to be able to prove the facts beyond a shadow of doubt because they are not going to believe you.
She said, "I have a 35mm camera with a wide-angle lens and a tripod. You are welcome to use it."

So, I got her camera and set it up in a window upstairs to where it couldn't be seen outside of the house.

I had to come home from work one day to take Jamie to the doctor. I usually parked my truck in the back when I was home, but for some reason this time I parked out front.

When I came through the front door, Carolyn told me that the boy was over there. I ran upstairs and looked through the camera. What I saw had me shaking so badly I couldn't even snap the camera. I went down and told Carolyn what had happened. She said maybe I could get Julie to take the pictures, so I showed Julie how to work the camera.

I took the film to the photoshop where I knew a guy, and told him what was in the film. I needed those pictures to prove what I was going to tell his daddy. A couple of days later, I came in after work and Carolyn said that Julie got the pictures back from the developer.

I waited until I knew he was home, walked over there, and called him outside. I told his father that I only took the pictures because I didn't want him to doubt what I was going to tell him. I made it clear that the only thing I wanted was for this to stop, and that it would be the end of it.

He said he would take care of it.

The next day the boy's mother got three of her family members together and they sat on the porch and stared over at our house all day. I told Carolyn that it didn't seem like it was taken care of.

Things escalated. Boys at school started coming up to Julie and saying dirty stuff to her. I called the principal, but it didn't stop. Julie ended up quitting school halfway through her senior year. The decision for Julie to quit school came after the boy's brother jumped on Julie and beat her in the face after they got off the bus one day.

My uncle was the bus driver, and I called him to ask if he would go and tell the principal, but he said he didn't want to get involved in something like that.

*****

Carolyn decided to go over to St. Albans Hospital and check herself in. She wanted them to start her on a medicine for the panic attacks that had developed from the situation. Julie went as well, maybe to be sure her mommy would go, but also for her weight.

They started Carolyn on Xanax. I would go over there every day after work to see them. I kept telling Carolyn every day that I believed she was getting worse. I tried to get her to come home. She said she wanted to give the medicine enough time to see if it would help her.

I came home one night, and I called a former pastor and trusted friend that I had helped build the Faith Temple Church. He told me that I needed to get by myself, pour my heart out to God, and just tell Him what is going on.

I got a blanket that night and lay down on the living room floor. Jamie was staying with Carolyn's sister, so it was just me and the Lord. I started to pray.

I began to speak in other tongues, falling asleep that night while speaking. The next morning, I awoke and went to work.

At about 8:30 am, somebody hollered at me and said I had a phone call. When I answered the phone, it was Denisse, Carolyn's friend. She said Carolyn called her and said she wanted me to go to get her, that she was ready to come home.

God was still answering my prayers.

Julie decided to stay for a while though and finish their weight program.

We decided to get Julie a new car. So, we went to Shelor's and bought her a new blue Cavalier and brought it home. We were going to give it to her once she left the hospital.

I parked it under the carport that evening. When I went outside the next morning, I couldn't believe my eyes. Someone had scratched up the whole hood on the car with a sharp object.

I called the police, and they said there was nothing they could do unless we saw who had done it.

This was just the beginning of harassment we faced for over 20 years. Looking back now, it amazes me how God works when you depend on Him.

Julie's Blue Cavalier

As the harrassment continued, I relied on God and his care of me and my family in numerous ways. Almost every morning when I was ready to leave for work, I would have a flat tire on one vehicle or another. I called the police again and again, but that was a waste of time. I laid outside night after night, hour after hour, watching for them. I realize now that it's probably a good thing that I didn't catch them.

*****

My mom and dad lived in Pearisburg. One day, Daddy went to a house they were tearing down in Narrows. He got a truck load of boards to use for kindling in the woodstove. This boy's daddy showed up at my father's door with a receipt from a garage where he had nails in all four tires of his vehicle. The man claimed that boards fell off of Daddy's truck, busting all four tires.

*****

One evening after work I had to go to the post office to mail a package for Carolyn. While I was in the office my phone rang. It was Carolyn, she said that my sister Betty and her two kids had been in a wreck, and she didn't know any details. It was only about two blocks from where I was. I told her I would call when I found out anything.

When I got there, they had Eric on the lawn in front of the doctor's office working with him. They were trying to bring him back. They worked on him for about two hours. They had taken Betty and Michelle to the hospital and they finally took Eric to the hospital. Michelle was okay and Betty was having x-rays. I was sitting in the waiting room when the doctor came out and he had a troubled look on his face. I walked over to him, and I told him I was Betty's brother.

He said they had opened Eric up and the aorta was torn off from his heart. I could tell he hated going in there and telling Betty. I asked him if he wanted me to go in there with him. When we walked through the door where she was, we didn't have to say a word, she just started screaming. Betty and Eric's dad were divorced, and he lived in California. When he came in for the funeral, I could see that he took the loss of his son really hard.

Eric's Dad had made the statement years before that his dream in life was to die from cirrhosis of the liver from drinking. He was a bartender and that is what he died with years later. Eric and Michelle always argued about who was going to ride "shotgun" in the front seat of the car. The day Eric won and got that seat, Betty pulled out and a car hit her antique Camaro in the passenger side door.

The guy was drunk, and he had been driving around town all day. The police had received several calls, but they had been unable to catch up with him. My brother also told me that Betty and her husband were arguing when she left before the wreck.

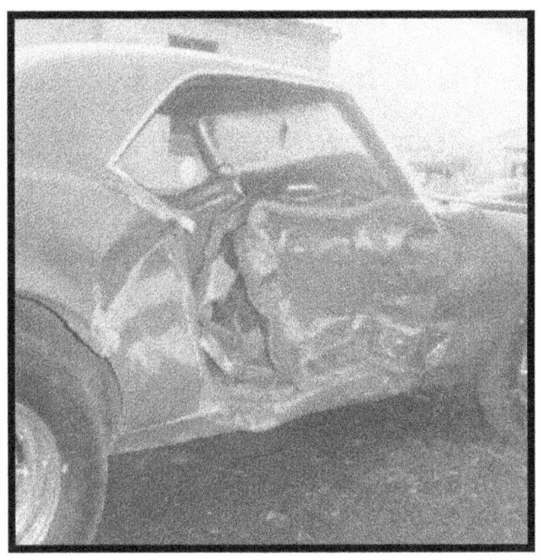

The car my nephew, Eric died in from the accident

Chapter 15:
Beach Trip

 Carolyn made arrangements with all her babysitting clients for a two-week hiatus, and as a bonus, we were able to leave a day early for our excursion. Everyone knew she deserved this trip, and they were happy for her.

We drove to Southern Georgia the first day and spent the night with her sister Joyce. The next day we drove on to Daytona Beach.

I put a mattress in the back of my Ford truck so Jamie could ride back there under the camper top. The breeze through the camper windows, along with the bedding, provided a comfortable place to lie down and sleep part of the time. I took Route 1 from Georgia to Daytona. While we were going through Jacksonville, Carolyn had fallen asleep. A big bridge that went up in the air was along the route, and while we were crossing it, she opened her eyes and couldn't see anything but blue sky. She was instantly terrified and let out a scream.

Once we got to the motel, it was packed. I told Carolyn I didn't want to stay there in such a dangerous place. Before we left Narrows, I had bought a .32 caliber Derringer double barrel pistol. I kept it in the truck but put it in my front pocket to take it into the motel room with us.

Carolyn said that we had already paid the deposit and probably wouldn't get it back. I could only agree to try it, but told her if it gets rough, we will go and find another motel.

The front desk attendant put us up on the fourth floor. Someone was beating on our door four to five times that night. I went down the next morning and talked to the manager. He said he would move us down to the ground floor if we stayed.

The hotel pool was also a point of contention for us. A time limit was posted prohibiting any swimming after 11 pm. People were jumping off the diving board all night long, keeping us awake.

I told Carolyn "I don't believe these people have ever seen a swimming pool before".

The next morning, I went to see the manager again. I told him we were leaving. He said that all these people are college students from Georgia. They would be gone the next day. He said, "After they leave, you couldn't ask for a better place to stay."

We drove to Disney World, Sea World and Kennedy Space Center, enjoying all the sites and venues.

Jamie-Kennedy Space Center, Florida

The only thing I didn't like about Daytona was that they let people drive on the beach. It did not feel safe for families and especially children with vehicles going by constantly. In total, we were at the beach for eight days and overall had a great time. Finally, it was time to leave though, and we still had to stop by Joyce's house, Carolyn's sister, to install storm windows for her before heading towards home.

We came back up Interstate 95 then traveled onto Interstate 16, headed to Statesboro. This took about five hours. Carolyn's family had said a tornado had hit the area while we were gone. It came close but it didn't do any damage. The next morning, I started the windows. It wasn't long until my stomach started hurting. About the time I would get up on the ladder, I would have to come down and go to the bathroom. I struggled to get the windows up. It took me about two days. We were aiming to come home after I got the windows up, but I was afraid to attempt driving. If I were on the interstate and have to go to the bathroom, I would be in a pickle.

I couldn't eat anything but cheese and crackers, and we ended up staying until the end of the week.

Joyce went to the drug store and got me some medicine. The time came and we had to go, and I made it home well enough. I stopped in the northern part of North Carolina and got a cheeseburger and fries. The next morning, I had diarrhea again and went to see my doctor. He said I had probably got a virus from the pool in Florida. It was about six months before I completely got over it. I was happy that Carolyn had made the trip, as she had been housebound for seven years.

Chapter 16:
Lerona, West Virginia &
More Construction

Brother Furrow had built a new Pentecostal church in Lerona, West Virginia, in 1988. A woman from there had been calling Carolyn inviting us to come for a visit. It was about an hour drive, so I decided to go. They were surprised to see me sporting my long beard, and it was the only time I have grown one.

The next Sunday, Carolyn, Jamie and I went to the church in Lerona for Sunday School and church services. We would spend the next two years attending there, and would drive the hour trip each way four to five times a week.

In January, Carolyn and I started talking about redoing the outside of the house. What we aimed to do was install new windows and put vinyl siding on the outside of the house. So, I went to the credit union and borrowed $25,000. I guess I gave Carolyn that snowball on the top of the mountain and then she rolled it over the side. The further it went, the

The house before remodeling

bigger that snowball got. I told David, my grandson's Daddy, that if he helped me re-do the house, I would give him the Ford truck. He was very excited about that.

First, I changed all the plumbing and then put in new sewer and water lines all the way down to the street. Then we decided to move the washer and dryer from the basement to the first floor so she wouldn't have to go up and down the steps to do laundry. I thought, if I was building a new bathroom, I'd build a new bath with a shower, so she wouldn't have to go upstairs to take a bath or a shower.

To accomplish all of this, I built a laundry room, hallway and a full bathroom where the back porch had been. Then Carolyn said it would be nice if we had a big front porch, so I started that construction next.

After this, I noticed some people coming by to see how much our home was changing. I was still working forty hours a week at the plant, so I had to do the house construction during the evenings, weekends and during vacation time. I had five weeks of vacation, so I spent all of my time off from my full-time job on the house.

I started David on the digging, which unfortunately did not work out too well. My neighbor told me that he would come by our house five or six times a day and never caught the man working; mostly sitting around a lot, the neighbor said. David had his brother help him.

I had to do most of the digging. I hated letting him go after I told him I would give him the truck. I figured I'd try to make it the best I could. I told David's brother that I didn't have the money to pay him, and I had made a deal with him for the truck. He said that he was just helping his brother out.

There were other complications with the construction. I ran into a rock in the footer that was bigger than a car hood. I dug under it and tried using an eight-foot timber as leverage, but it wouldn't move. So, I poured my footer and laid the block up to the sides of the rock. I had put casing under the porch so if anyone later had to change a water pipe or sewer line, they could just pull the pipe out without having to disturb anything.

David worried me, wanting the title of the truck to be signed over to him. He said, "I won't quit on you," but as soon as I gave him the title, he disappeared.

Once I got the block laid, I had to fill the porch up with rocks. It was hard to believe how much rock I dug out of the footers. I got a huge amount of rock out where I built the bathroom and utility room on the back too. People would stop and ask me where I got all those rocks, and they couldn't believe it was from there. I ordered all my material and put it in the shop, so I didn't have to wait for anything. I formed up the porch and steps for the concrete. I ordered a tandem truck load of gravel to finish filling the porch and bring it up to grade. I built a ramp on the end to roll the gravel in a wheelbarrow.

I told Carolyn that it looked like I'd need to roll all that gravel in there and she said, "Didn't you make a deal with David when you gave him the truck?" I could only answer that yes, that was the deal, but David had flown the coop on me.

She went in there and called David, she told him "You better be down here and put that gravel in the porch or I am going to take the truck back." The next day, he and his brother showed up and put all the gravel in the porch. When I came from work that evening, he wouldn't even look at me. They finished the gravel and just left.

I asked my niece's husband to pour the concrete for me and spent a whole day forming up my steps, because I didn't want any of the structure to give. He poured the concrete that evening.

*****

During this time, we started cleaning the church every week. The Church bought a Volkswagen van, and I started taking the kids Carolyn was keeping to church. Now I knew exactly how they felt when they were making all those trips to Pearisburg every week.

They gave me the job of teaching the teens' Sunday School class. I had taught a lot of Sunday School classes, but the teen class was the most challenging. They were curious and they weren't afraid to ask questions.

It was a blessing to Carolyn and I, but it was hard doing everything I was involved in.

Brother Furrow called me one night and told me he wanted a cross in front of the sanctuary. It was a three-dimensional view of a cross, about five feet tall with a light behind it, mounted on a frame that would not be visible from the front. He wanted it made from black walnut. I told him we would look at it when I came up there the next time. He said, "I knew if it could be done that you were the only one who could do it." I told him it would be an honor for me to build it.

I built the cross, took it up there one evening after work, and put it up.

Cross made from black walnut

It was beautiful. The pastor kept sitting there on the pew looking at the cross. I finally told him that he could sit and look at it as long as he wanted but that I was tired, and I was going home. He wanted to know what he owed me, and I said that it was nothing, that Jesus would take care of me.

One Wednesday evening, I had worked several shifts of overtime the preceding days, and I didn't feel like driving. Carolyn took the car and several of the kids she was keeping and went to church in Lerona. Later, she called and told me she had run into the back of a pickup truck in Athens. I went over to a U-Haul place, rented a trailer and went to the church to get my car. When I got there, the church was empty. No one was around, so I came back home. When I got back, the car was sitting in the driveway. Carolyn said Brother Furrow had checked the car and said it was okay to drive. He had let church out early to allow her to drive back before dark. It would have been better if I had gone with my family; that was where I was supposed to be.

*****

Brother Furrow was a good carpenter. He had built three churches already. He called and asked me if I could plane a load of lumber for him. I told him to bring it down one evening.

We were way after dark getting it planed, and my neighbors were always just looking for some reason to call the police on me. They would call the cops on me for creating too much dust, noise or even somebody parking in the alley. I had a commercial dust collector and an air cleaner that filtered the air I breathed.

Usually when the police showed up, I would tell them to go and to tell the neighbors to kiss my rear end. Of course, they would say they wouldn't do that because even the police were afraid of them. Everybody was afraid of them, well, except one crazy old Marine. I knew I was right and had the pictures to prove what was going on in the house across the street, but I didn't want to ruin someone's life.

I had burnt wood for heat for the past eight years. I had a big stove built by someone at the plant who was very skilled at this kind of work. It would keep my whole house warm, all three floors. I only had to put wood in it every eight hours.

When I worked overtime, I would call and tell Carolyn not to forget to put wood in the stove and I would call back at supper time and remind her. When I came in at 11 pm my fire would be out, and the house would be cold. She would have the oven turned on in the kitchen trying to get warm. I would have to cut kindling and start a fire.

I finally got tired of fighting the battle and hired a coworker, who did this work on the side, to put in a gas furnace, a heat pump and a duct system. I had to go to the credit union and borrow the money. It was nice and I didn't have to worry about the wood anymore. I still burnt wood for heat in the shop. Plus, it was a perfect way to get rid of my scrap wood.

The wood shavings that come out of the dust collector were saved for the people at work. They would put them in their garden. One day I cleaned the dust collector and set the bags out beside the shop. I would tell them when I had bags ready and they would come and pick them up.

I went to work and told someone that I had five trash bags of shavings. I came home that evening and my shavings were gone. It amazes me when you keep your mind turned to God where he will take you. I couldn't figure out what had happened to my shavings. Did someone steal them or did the town pick them up? I had been doing this for years and nothing had ever happened to them.

I called the Town, and they said they didn't get them. There was a man who lived by himself at the end of the alley. He was the retired plant manager of the Appalachian Power Plant in Glen Lyn. I had never been to the man's house, but he was always friendly when I passed by him.

I was supposed to take Carolyn and the kids that evening to Pearisburg to Walmart. I was still trying to figure out what had happened to my shavings. I thought maybe Mr. Ratcliff at the end of the alley might have seen somebody get them. I went out in the yard, and it was like something just dragged me to go to his house and ask him. I never left without telling Carolyn where I was going. I never thought about that this time, I just went.

When I got there his car was in the driveway. I went to the front door, and the inside door was open. I pecked on the storm door several times, but no one answered. I thought that maybe he didn't hear me, so I went around the house to the kitchen door. Again, there was no response even when the inside door was open. I looked through the door and saw what appeared to be a foot on the kitchen floor. I opened the storm door and went in.

Mr. Ratcliff was lying on the floor in front of the sink. His pants were wet where he peed on himself. He could talk a little and said he had been lying there for about three hours.

He didn't act like he could move anything on his left side. I called 911 and told them what I had found. They said that help was on the way.

I asked the old man if there was anyone I could call, and he said he had a son in Princeton and he was able to give me the number. I called his son and told him who I was and what happened to his dad. It was just a little while until two ambulances came rolling in. The EMTs said he had a stroke and it was a miracle I found him, or he would probably have died.

I pray that if something like that ever happens to me, God will send someone along to find me. I never saw Mr. Ratcliff again nor did anyone ever say thank you. I heard that he was in a nursing home, and they sold his house.

Chapter 17:
Daddy Got Sick

Daddy got sick and went to the Giles County emergency room. He had never been to the doctor in his life and it must have felt terrible giving in and going. He thought he had the flu, but after a lot of tests they found out that he needed triple bypass surgery, and he had diabetes.

For years, he had worked for Birchlawn Cemetery, but now wasn't able to anymore. They were treating him at Giles Hospital where there was a visiting heart doctor that came there occasionally. Daddy got to where he couldn't carry an armful of wood to put in the stove.

The doctor finally decided they would send him to Roanoke Memorial Hospital. They had a heart team there and could do heart surgeries twenty-four hours a day. I took a vacation day and went down there to spend the day with him. We did a lot of talking while I sat with him. He told me that he couldn't go to his own father's funeral because of the way he beat him when he was growing up. I learned so many things I never knew about my Dad and we talked like we never had before.

Roanoke Memorial would not do the surgery because of his diabetes and they also didn't think he was strong enough to get through it. Daddy said he didn't want to lie in that bed until he died. However, the doctors would try to send him to the University of Virginia (UVA) Hospital if they would agree to do the surgery, he told me. About two days later, he was enroute to UVA; they had given him a date for the surgery. He had been in Roanoke for thirty days.

He wanted all of his kids to be there the day of the surgery, which was scheduled for early in the morning, so we left home at 1 am. We wanted to make sure we got there so we could see him before they took him. His sister was there from California, and my sister Betty rode with me.

When we got there, we went straight to his room and they were prepping him for surgery.. Mommy didn't go, as she was not the type of person to leave home very often. Daddy looked at me and smiled, they gave him a shot, and then he started to sleep.

I went down to the chapel several times that day, knelt and prayed for him. It was a long day but finally the doctor came to the waiting room and told us that he had come through the surgery and was doing well. The medical staff would let him sleep until the next day and we were welcome to stay but we wouldn't get to talk to him until then. I told everybody I was going back home, and it would serve no purpose to sit there all night. Everyone agreed.

I had to go to the lumber plant the next day to get something for the pool. When I came back, Carolyn told me that they had called from the hospital. Daddy had passed away. Post-surgery he had a leak, we didn't know where, but they were in the process of opening him up to put an artificial heart in when they lost him.

It was four days later when I remember sitting there at Daddy's funeral and looking at him in the coffin-strange thoughts came to mind. I thought to my-self "wouldn't it be something if he would sit up there in that coffin?"

I also remembered that night when he went to church with me and the pastor never even gave an altar call. He never went back to church again.

I had prayed with him, but I don't know for sure that he asked Jesus to come into his heart. I hope so. As the saying goes, never put off until tomorrow what you can do today. Tomorrow may never come. So, anyone who may be reading this and you are not saved, don't put it off until tomorrow.

The owners of Birchlawn gave Mommy plots for her and Daddy. They didn't charge him anything for the opening and closing. My sister Violet had worked for them for years along with our father. Daddy told Mommy before he passed away that if anything ever happened to him, do not let a certain mortician have his body, and she knew who.

Years ago, Daddy worked for this man and dug all the graves by hand, only receiving $50 a grave in pay. Daddy had also cut several big trees for this man at the funeral home that were right beside the street. It would have cost him a fortune to get them cut by someone else.

Daddy asked him several times for his money and the mortician always said he didn't have his checkbook with him and that he would pay him later. He never did. So, Mommy got Givens Funeral Home to take care of Daddy.

Chapter 18:
Working for a Living

It was about this time I noticed that the new hires at work were different than what we had previously known. The hourly people they were hiring were arrogant and all they wanted to do was kiss the staff's rear ends.

They had closed a plant in Cumberland, Maryland and some of the staff from there were transferred to our location. Then, they closed a plant in Rome, Georgia and we got some more staff from there too.

I had based my life on honesty. Everyone who knew me would know what I stood for and that I was a Christian.

One day someone put a paper on the bulletin board about something. I don't remember what it was about, but it had real dirty language on it. Someone told the foreman that I was the one who put it up there.

The foreman told him "You are wrong on that big boy; I have known Richard for years and I have never heard a dirty word come out of his mouth."

I had never been in a place where people would do anything they could if they thought it would give them a few points with the foreman. I saw a lot of people come and go. Most of the foremen we got didn't last long. They would be there for a few years and then they would be gone for one reason or another.

They asked me a few times if I would take a promotion and I said no. I thought you would have to be a first-class liar to have a foreman's job and I'm not interested.

To compound the stress our family was experiencing, it happened around this time that a woman had run a stop sign and hit Julie in her vehicle, hurting her back. I told her not to sign a release with the insurance company. She didn't listen. She signed the release for a little bit of money.

Julie was working at a nursing home in Lindside, West Virginia, and told me that they were making them lift residents by themselves. A doctor put her on Xanax, the same medicine Carolyn was taking.

Julie and her husband, Allen

Julie, her first-born Terrance, and Allen

Julie, her daughter Cambrea, and Allen

Chapter 19:
Our Pigeon Forge Friends

We started going to Pigeon Forge every weekend, leaving on Fridays and coming back on Sundays. Carolyn and I were both Elvis fans and there was a guy at Memories Theater in Pigeon Forge that looked and sounded just like him.

Most of the time I would work two or three shifts overtime throughout the week and would leave work early on Friday. We would get to Pigeon Forge in time to catch a show at 8 pm.

We got to know Eddie, the Elvis impersonator, and his wife Doris pretty well after Carolyn went up one night after the show to meet Eddie. I built several cabinets for them. One in particular I constructed was made from red oak to display a set of twelve Elvis plates they had received from someone.

I talked on the phone several times with them, and they told me what they wanted. It was hard to get them on the phone sometimes. I would call the theatre, explain who I was and who I needed to talk to. Doris would then come to the phone.

Carolyn and I, and the cabinet I made

The cabinet I built for them was beautiful. I made two guitars out of oak and mounted one on each side.

Carolyn and I took the cabinet to them on one of our vacation trips. We had to take the truck, so we put the cabinet in the back along with a small mattress. Jamie and Crystal, my sister's girl, rode in the back too.

As we got closer to Pigeon Forge, my brakes on the truck didn't feel just right. When I pulled into the parking lot at Memories Theatre, my brake pedal went all the way to the floor. It was a miracle they didn't go out on the interstate. I wasn't aiming to give them the cabinet until after the show that night but now everything had changed. I went inside and asked if I could talk to Eddie. They said he was in rehearsal. About that time, Doris walked by. I told her what was going on, and she said she would get him. When they saw what was in the truck, they loved it. We took it inside to put in his dressing room.

He told me to call Carr's Garage and to tell them that he had sent me. I did and it wasn't but a few minutes until a wrecker showed up. I told Carolyn that I had to go with the truck so they could stay there at the theatre until I got back.

The truck was fixed before the show started that night.

Carolyn told me that a woman at the theatre next door took them to the motel and came back to the show. Her name was Gail Ballinger. She worked at a theater beside Memories Smokey Mountain Jubilee in the ticket booth, and she would give us a discount every time we went to the show. We would go there for the daytime show and go to Memories at night.

Carolyn-Pigeon Forge, Tennessee

Chapter 20:
A New Way to Travel

I bought a 23-foot camper from a man in Giles County. The camper was like new, and I paid $10,000 for it. The man I bought it from pulled it to Pigeon Forge for me. I left it down there all the time as the RV park only charged me $2.00 a night to store it.

Our Camper RV

When we stayed there, I would call to let them know we were coming, and they would put the camper in a spot for us. If they didn't need the space, they would just leave it parked, and then it only cost $10 a night for Carolyn, Jamie and me to stay there. We really liked it. It was a lot better than staying in a motel. However, I learned a lot about RVs over time, some lessons are a little more dangerous than others.

When we arrived at the RV park, I only had to hook up the electric, and the sewer and water hoses. One day, I was changing the propane tank, and I didn't realize that gas had built up in the compartment where the gas tank sat. When I lit the pilot light, a ball of fire blew out of the hole and just missed my head.

God was still watching out for me.

We had never been to the Grand Ole Opry in Nashville, Tennessee, so we decided to get tickets for Saturday night and go. We also found out that there was a concert at Viking Hall in Bristol on Sunday night, so I called and got tickets as well.

The concerts showcased major entertainers George Jones, Conway

Twitty and Billy Jo Royal. I told Carolyn that this would probably be the last time we would ever be able to see all three of them in concert.

The concert tickets were purchased about three months in advance, giving us plenty of time to make plans. We thought we would leave early on Friday and drive part of the way on Friday evening, then spend the night somewhere, and go the rest of the way on Saturday morning. We also planned to drive back to Bristol on Sunday and make it to a concert on Sunday night.

As things tend to happen when you have plans, the week we were going on our trip, some equipment broke down at my job, and I had to work over three nights on the 11 pm-7 am shifts. Then I worked daylight. I figured I'd be okay to drive though.

I left work on Friday at about 2 pm, came home and we already had everything ready to go.

I knew I was tired so I got a washcloth and laid it on the dash so I could wipe my face if I got sleepy. I told Carolyn to keep an eye on me and make sure I didn't start to doze. I wiped my face a couple times with the washcloth.

Somewhere between Wytheville and Bristol I was doing about 70 mph and I didn't realize that something suddenly had started to happen. I had slipped into a state between asleep and awake. Carolyn startled me awake letting out a scream. They were working on a bridge, and the traffic had stopped.

I threw my foot on the brake. The only thing I could figure is that God stopped that van. The vehicle behind me slid, and to avoid hitting me, swerved and ran up beside me. That was about the dumbest decision I had ever made, working that much overtime and planning a trip like that. I ruined the whole weekend.

We went on to Knoxville and then to Crossville, Tennessee, where we spent the night. The next morning, we drove into Nashville. It was November, so it was cold. We got a motel room at Days Inn, not far from the Grand Ole Opry. This was the last day the amusement park would open. I told Carolyn and Jamie that they couldn't stand it out there in the cold. So, we hung around the motel and took a nap, then got up and went out to eat.

I didn't think I was going to get Carolyn in there. She said she was having trouble breathing in the cold air, but we finally made it, and we really enjoyed the Grand Ole Opry. We got up on Sunday morning and drove back to Bristol and found another motel room that wasn't too far from Viking Hall. We decided to locate the concert hall so we would know where we were going later for the show.

That evening we got ready and left about an hour before time for the concert to start. I had to park a good ways from the entrance, and as we started walking towards the door Carolyn said she couldn't go any further. She was having trouble breathing.

I said, "you got to be kidding me". We were in sight of the door to the concert hall.

I told her I'd take her and Jamie to the motel and then I'd go back to watch the concert. She said "No, you're not going to leave me anywhere".

We went back to the motel, but I didn't speak to her for about six months. Finally, I gave in and started talking to her. It just hurt so bad because I had waited for months to see that concert. I still have the tickets for the show. They were never used.

Chapter 21:
Relatives, Romance and Rendezvous

My sister's girl was having trouble with her boyfriend, and she had a little boy. He was about three years old, and his mother didn't want to take care of him. We agreed to take him in for a while and treated him just as if he was ours.

Along with taking him to Pigeon Forge with us on trips, one day we decided to take him to the Knoxville Zoo. He walked the whole way through, and it took us about a half day to get to see the park When he returned home to his mother, we hated to see him go as we had become so attached to the little fellow. Now he only lives about a block from us.

*****

Julie now had a new boyfriend. She brought him by the house one night and introduced him to me. He was a few years younger than her, but he was a nice-looking boy.

He didn't have a job, so I asked him to help me do some work. I was building a garage on the side of my shop and had to hang two 13-foot steel doors. I explained to him that he should be careful as you could get your fingers mashed. I noticed that he was looking towards the house a lot to see if he could see Julie. I reminded him several times about getting his fingers mashed in the doors. This wasn't my first rodeo. It wasn't long until he let out a scream. I had moved the door, and it got his fingers. He felt that lesson for a few days.

*****

A lot of the women that came to see Eddie at the Memories Theater would just throw themselves at him in the same way women did with Elvis.

Eddie ended up having an affair with his boss' wife. She was a beautiful woman; however, I couldn't understand how a man that was making as much money as he did would mess up his life like that. His boss had made him half owner in the theater.

So naturally, Eddie was leaving the theater. I had previously made two 20-inch by 30-inch red oak picture frames, installed Eddie's picture in them, and hung the frames in the theater's lobby. I asked Eddie if I could have the picture with him in a red jump suit and he said yes. One evening he and Doris brought that picture down to the motel and gave it to me. I had also made a frame for the hotel manager and he never charged for a night's stay.

After Eddie left the theater, Carolyn got discouraged about going to Pigeon Forge. She said that if we weren't using the camper every week, we needed to sell it. I got the man that had taken it down there for me to go bring it back. I tried my best to give him $200 for going to get it, but he would only take $50 for the gas. I put an ad in the newspaper and sold it for the same thing I had given for it.

We still went to Pigeon Forge from time to time. Someone else came into the theater and did the act for the Elvis show. We went to see the show one night and about a quarter of the way through, we got up and walked out. It just wasn't as good as Eddie.

Julie came with us to Pigeon Forge again, and I took her up in a helicopter. She surprised me with how much she loved it.   Jamie wanted to go but Carolyn wouldn't let her. She told her that only when she is 18 years old, then she can make her own decisions.

Chapter 22:
A New Family Member

We were still doing a lot of traveling at this time, so I wanted to buy a high-top van. I went over to Shelor's Dealership in Christiansburg. I found a van that I just fell in love with. It was a white and teal green high-top luxury model. I called Carolyn to see what she thought and she liked the idea. The car salesman and I spent the whole day negotiating the terms of the purchase and I must have called Carolyn about ten times. The salesman told me that he had made a lot of sales but that was the hardest sale he had ever made. I took it home and Carolyn just loved it. The van had a full-size bed in the back if you let the seat down.

Through the next year we went to Myrtle beach five times. Carolyn liked to get in the back and lay down. She would bring her pillow and a blanket and that is where she would spend most of the trip.

Sometimes we would go to Myrtle Beach and spend a few days then go to Georgia to Joyce's house and stay a night or two. Then we would go to Pigeon Forge. Carolyn would lie in the bed throughout the trip.

When I got off the interstate, I told her we were almost there, and Carolyn sat up. About the time she was getting up, a red light appeared ahead and there was a car in front of me. The light turned red and the car throwed his brakes on, and I had to lock it up to keep from hitting the car's bumper. Carolyn started running towards the front of the van. I could see her through the mirror. I put my hand out and caught her by the forehead to keep her from running her head into the dash of the van. Good thing Jesus was riding with us.

\

*****

Julie was still dating David and working at the nursing home. It was then she told us she was pregnant. In my opinion, no daddy likes to hear that when their children aren't married. I prayed for them and just did the best I could to provide support. She was still having a lot of trouble with her back and living with us. I was concerned, but I knew God would take care of us no matter what. Sometimes it takes a lot of trust.

David got a job at the lumber plant, working at the front as a cashier. Julie worked a few more months and then she took off. She rented a house from Joyce, Carolyn's sister, so she and David started living there.

Finally, the day came, it was time for the baby. It was a big baby boy, and she named him Terrance McKinley Martin. When she came home from the hospital, she stayed with us so she could be with Carolyn who would help her take care of Terrance. David stayed at their house.

It didn't take long to get attached to the baby. I had a big recliner and that was where Terrance would go to sleep at night. After a couple of weeks, she decided she was going home to be with David.

I had second thoughts about her taking care of the baby. She took him home with her but after a couple of days, she came back and said he was too much trouble to take care of. She wanted us to keep him for a while.

We treated him just like he was one of our own. It didn't take long until we had him spoiled rotten. He wasn't but a month or two old until we took him on a trip to Tennessee.

Chapter 23:
Jamie's Christmas Present

That coming Christmas, Jamie was going to be 16 years old. I stopped at Newberry Ford one evening and saw they had a red Ford Mustang that was a demo. I came home and told Carolyn what I had on my mind, and she liked the idea. I would get it for Jamie as a Christmas present.

I bought the car, and the dealer kept it until a few days before Christmas. Eventually I brought it home and put it in the garage. My garage had a 13-foot steel roll-up door on both ends. She was in school when I brought it home, so she wouldn't see the surprise. I also put dark paper over the windows so she couldn't see in the garage, and bought a really nice key ring for her.

It was tradition for us to open presents on Christmas Eve. So, we opened presents like we always did, and I chose that moment to sneak outside and open the garage door facing the house. I cut the lights out so she could see into the garage.

I came back into the house about the time they were finished opening presents. Someone said "I guess that's all" but I said no, there was another one. I walked to Jamie and handed her the keys. She just looked puzzled. I told her to look out the door. When she saw the car, she turned white as a sheet. She couldn't believe what she saw. The garage had enough light in there that it was brighter than day. By the time she finished drivers' education and got her permit, she had a new car to drive.

One night, while driving the Mustang, Jamie had a close call. I was working overtime and Carolyn called me on the job. She said that Jamie went to Pearisburg and was on her way back when a black bear ran across the road in front of her. It scared her so bad that she was still crying when she got home. I feel she had an angel of protection with her that night.

Chapter 24:
The Drug Bust

I'm going to tell you about the next episode of my life, but will not reveal names because that is not important. I just want to show what happened and the way God took care of my family and I during this period.

Jamie, Carolyn, Terrance and I were sitting in Christiansburg at Burger King eating when the restaurant's phone rang. Normally I wouldn't pay any attention to a phone ringing but this time it got my attention. I didn't know it was for me, and I can't explain why it got my attention, but it felt like the call would somehow be for me.

The girl behind the counter yelled "Is there a Richard Perdue here?" I thought who in the world could that be if no one knew we were there.

I answered the call, and it was Julie. I asked her how she knew where we were, and she just said she knew I liked to eat there. She also said I would never believe what just happened. I said I'd believe anything. She said, "A deputy just brought three warrants to the door for mommy, for selling drugs".

There had to be a mistake, Carolyn wouldn't do something like that. I almost fell on the floor. I told Julie that I had just cashed a large check at the Credit Union for a job I was getting ready to do and they had paid me for the material. Thoughts were running through my mind by then. I was worried and I was mad; I didn't know the next step.

If they were watching Carolyn and pulled me over they might think it was drug money, I said to Julie. So, my daughter and I decided to meet between the restaurant and home. I would give her the money, and until I could drive home, she could keep it. I asked her to not tell me where she was going to meet me, but she still said, "I'll meet you at Ron's Stop and Shop."

I refused.

They told Julie to tell Carolyn to go to the sheriff's office and turn herself in. I went back to the booth and sat down, and Carolyn asked what happened.

I told her what Julie said to me, and she went into silent mode. The more she stayed silent the angrier I got.

It's amazing how the Holy Spirit brings peace in times like these. I kept trying to get information from her, but she wouldn't talk. I was imagining everything. I said I had to take her to the Sheriff's office, but she said, "I'm not going there".

I said she was going one way or another.

We went to the Sheriff, and they allowed me to go with her to be fingerprinted. I asked the deputy what this was all about. He was a real smart aleck. He said it was for selling drugs.

I thought to myself, this would ruin our whole lives. God says to be patient but that was really hard in a situation like this. When we got home, I figured it was time for some real answers. I told Carolyn I didn't know what was going on and that I couldn't help her unless she said something. She finally told me what had happened.

A woman Carolyn babysat for, who would come in every evening to get her kids, would give her a hard luck story about how depressed she was. Carolyn was someone who would give you the shirt off her back. She just had a tender heart.

So, Carolyn gave this woman a Xanax a few evenings. It wasn't long until her low-life boyfriend wanted one too. She gave him one a few times and finally she told him she couldn't give her the pills because she had to pay for them. He said not to worry that he could pay for them. Carolyn didn't realize they were setting her up. She had not told me anything about what happened before. If she had, maybe I could have stopped this nonsense. Although, I might have been the one that would be sent to jail.

With the help of the Lord, I started to figure some things out.

I told Carolyn; "I'm going to tell you just how it is. I love you with all my heart. I am going to do everything I can to get you out of this mess, but I am going to make you a promise. If you ever do anything like this again in your lifetime, I will walk away so quick it will make your head spin."

Details of what happened had started coming to my mind. This low-life guy had got into trouble with an underage girl. The woman Carolyn babysat for knew about what happened with our neighbors previously and had gone to the police chief with information. He made a deal that he could get Carolyn for drugs if they would cut time off his sentence.

Don't ever let your guard down, if you do, the devil will come after you. I was nice to this boy. I had enough evidence to prosecute him, but I didn't want to hurt him. I know boys will make mistakes. My job has always been to win souls not to hurt anyone.

I could have kept him out of the fire department, and out of the police department.

When I had given his dad the pictures, he told me he would take care of the situation. That was before the mother got the news. I think she is the one that caused all the problems.

When I got up the next morning, there was a knock on my front door. I looked across the street and there was a spotlight shining at the front of my house. At closer examination, I could see a camera pointed at the door and a reporter. I didn't go outside and finally they left.

When I went to work, it was on every local radio station and television. I got newspapers and the story was in all of them. I called the Sheriff's office and asked about all the publicity. They said they don't operate like that. I knew then the mother must have been alerting the news media.

On my job, I went into the break room one day and one of the men I worked with asked me if I knew who the woman down in Narrows was that got busted for drugs. The first thing that came to mind was to lie to him. The Holy Spirit in me said to tell the truth, and that he was going to find out anyway. It hurt me, but I said it was my wife.

Someone recommended a lawyer over in Dublin, so I called and got an appointment to talk to him. When we went to the law office, they had us fill out a paper before you went in to talk to the lawyer. It didn't take me long to figure out what the paper was for. It was to find out how much money I had.

I didn't figure it was any of his business, but he wanted $10,000 to represent her. I told Carolyn that she had to pay the money out of funds her mother left her. So, the next morning she took that money in cash over there and paid for a 30-minute appearance in court.

They confined her for 90 days at home, and she even had to wear an ankle monitor. They also took her driving permit for one-and-a-half years. As part of the sentence, she had to also pay a fine, but I don't remember how much it was. That's a bad sentence for someone who has already been confined to the house for seven years.

There is more to this story, which will unfold later.

Carolyn and Richard

Chapter 25:
Grandbabies-Home to Stay

I talked Julie into giving me and Carolyn custody of Terrance. I told her I could put him on my insurance, and I was in a lot better shape to take care of him. She convinced David into going before the judge and giving up his rights to Terrance too. He agreed it was best for the boy.

Terrance and David

David also wanted a car, so we gave him $1500 for a down payment.

Julie continued to have a lot of trouble with her back and her nerves. She would go to St. Albans ever once a while and they would give her a shock treatment. I found out that she was buying painkillers from individuals. I chewed her out, but she said she knew what she was doing. I told her that she only thought she knew. That ate me like a cancer. I couldn't get it off my mind.

Several things happened during this time period. Julie broke up with David and started dating another man. We finally got past Carolyn's parole too, and she got her permit back. We could now leave the state of Virginia again, which had been part of her punishment.

Jamie, now a senior in high school, would sometimes have stiffness in her back. Someone told her she could pop her back to help, but I told her not to do that. She didn't listen.

One day Jamie popped her back and ruptured a disc. She was in so much pain she didn't feel like sitting in the classroom. I took her to our family doctor, but he wouldn't excuse her from school. Next, we brought Jamie to see a chiropractor, and she wrote an order to have her home schooled. The school sent a teacher to our house several times each week, which helped her a great deal.

It was also during this time that Jamie started dating John. Carolyn came to me one day to tell me that Jamie was pregnant. That just hurt me so badly. Jamie was my baby girl.

Jamie and John came to me one night and told me that they needed to talk. I told them I wasn't ready for this conversation; the moment I am ready I was going to reach out to them. Then I just walked away. They didn't know that Carolyn had already told me. About a week later, after I had prayed about the situation, I went to them.

John told me that they didn't mean this to happen, and they were sorry. I only could reply that what was done was done and there is nothing you can do about it now. I also told him "Jamie is my little girl, and I am going to make you a promise, that if you don't take care of her and if you ever mistreat her, there's not a rock on the face of the earth that you can hide under. I will find you". Now that I look back, I couldn't have found her a better husband.

I had kept both girls in church all their life so far and I guess I expected a lot from them. Every family has problems, but if we let Him, God will take care of the challenges that come our way.

However, Jamie faced another challenge; she couldn't have surgery on her back while she was pregnant. She had to endure the pain. The time came for her to have the baby, and we all went to the hospital. I felt so sorry for her being in labor with a ruptured disc. They gave her an epidural and that helped a lot. I prayed all along. Finally, Jamie made it through the ordeal, and the baby was healthy.

A week later I had a vacation scheduled to Myrtle Beach. We took Jamie and her new baby with us, a boy she and John named Brennan. We spent nine days there. John drove Jamie's mustang and came down there twice. He had to come back to work so he could not stay the whole trip. While we were at the beach, we went to see our friend Eddie every night.

One day Brennan's navel became sore and infected. We had to take him to the doctor. I had to pay for it out of my pocket. Jamie had Medicaid but it wouldn't pay for anything out of state.

Terrance liked riding in his car seat in the front of that big van. He loved to see the tractor trailers go by. We would walk along the beach early in the morning and collect seashells. We enjoyed the vacation, but the day came when we had to come home.

Allen was staying at the house with Julie. Joyce wanted me to build a bedroom addition to the house. Julie would sit there in the kitchen and look out the windows and watch cars go by.

Jamie, John and Brennan were living in our basement for a while until they could find a place of their own. It's hard for two families to live in the same house, but we made it work. I've always been accustomed to a crowd in the house with Carolyn's babysitting business.

I started to work on the house where Julie lived, and had to get a building permit for it. I started with the footers and the floor-all in one pour. Some of the rocks that came out of the footers were so big I had to roll them up a board to get them out.

Terrance was only about four, but I took him with me to work many times. I told him that after the building inspector came, I was going to roll the big rocks back into the footers and cover them with concrete.

The day I got the inspector to look at the footers, Terrance asked while he was there if we could roll the big rocks back. I thought to myself that I should have left him at home, but the inspector didn't seem to hear Terrance.

When I put up the rafters, I got someone to help me with the work. I could tell the guy was scared. I told him that if he was scared, he would end up falling, so I said, "I don't need you anymore" and paid him and let him go. I put the rest of the room up by myself. I was used to doing it like that.

I hired Allen to dig a bank around the back so the water would drain. When I got the room done, I had installed the door where Julie usually sat and looked out the window. She seemed more depressed after she could not look out the window anymore. Her and Allen ended up separating and she was alone.

Julie then found out she was pregnant and claimed it belonged to David and when she went to the hospital to have the baby, he was there with her.

They did bloodwork on the baby and discovered Allen was the father. The baby was a girl, and Julie named her Cambrea Jade Perdue. Looking back now, there's no way Allen could deny her because she is just like him.

Julie and Cambrea

Chapter 26:
My Child in Danger

Julie applied for HUD to get assistance paying her rent. She was approved, and then she and Cambrea moved into an apartment in Pearisburg. She didn't have anyone else to help her move. It was a job carrying all that stuff up the steps to the second floor. where she would live. We would also go there every evening and see what she needed from the store, and then get it for her.

It scared me to death to look up there and see Cambrea's little head sticking up from the bottom of the open window. Every time I would talk to Julie, I'd tell her about those open windows.

Julie got her a job somewhere over at Blacksburg, about 30 minutes from home. Carolyn was keeping Cambrea. One Friday she didn't come home from work. We had no idea where she was. Somebody told us on Saturday that they had seen her at Walmart with that low-life who had set Carolyn up. She went down on the river and stayed with him. That hurt me so bad I could have cried.

Later, this man would die in prison accused of molesting a child.

I worked in the shop and watched for Julie. Sunday evening, she came down the sidewalk beside the shop. I went outside to meet her and asked where she had been. She instantly started lying to me. She always had a problem keeping her mouth closed when I was trying to correct her.

I told her I couldn't believe that she would lower herself to go down there on the river and stay with that piece of trash. And even worse than that, go to Walmart where everybody could see her. She told me that I took her son and that we wouldn't take her daughter. I replied that I didn't have the intention to do so, but that I'll make sure that she would keep her daughter safe.

She kept running her mouth and I finally told her she had ten minutes to get her clothes, and get out of my house, or I'd throw her things out the window. Carolyn talked me into just leaving her alone and letting her stay. She stayed but she never went back to work. Sometimes she would stay in bed for two or three days and just get up to go to the bathroom.

Allen bought a trailer by Big Stoney Creek, close to where he worked at the lime plant. He moved all Julie's stuff out of the apartment. I was sure glad of that.

Chapter 27:
Truck Troubles

Carolyn, Terrance and I went down to Joyce's in Georgia. While we were down there, my son-in-law John called and asked if he could borrow my truck. He needed to get materials to work on his mother's house. I told him I didn't mind. John and Jamie were still staying there so he knew where the keys were.

When we came back after our vacation, I had a new kitchen to put in. John helped me install it.

One day, I was working by myself finishing up the kitchen job. I went to Dairy Queen to get lunch. While I was sitting there in the drive through waiting on food, I heard the engine making a clicking noise.

I finished the work I had to do and when I got home, I checked the oil. It was three quarts low. I didn't realize it was low when I went on vacation and John didn't know it was like that either. I filled it up and the truck sounded okay again.

The next Saturday, John called me to ask if he could use my truck again to go to Lowes and get materials for his mother's house. I told him it was fine.

I was working in the shop and my phone rang. John said something was wrong with the truck. It had become heated and then the engine stopped. I jumped in the van and went over there. The truck was dead, and the engine wouldn't even turn over. I told John that I was afraid the engine is gone.

I called the insurance company and gave them my location and told them that I needed a tow truck. We waited and waited. I called them back two or three times and asked them when the help would be there. It was about four hours before they arrived.

I had them tow the truck to the house and drop it off. I told John that I needed my truck, there was no way to run my shop without it. I had a lot of work to do. John said he would go with me to see if we could find a truck. We went to

Shelor's car lot in Christiansburg. They were about the biggest dealer around. I found one I liked, a 2002 white Dodge quad cab. I had been admiring them for some time.

It was getting close to time for them to close, so I went up to the showroom, and it so happened that I was able to speak to the manager. I asked him what he would take for that Dodge straight out. He said "you could have never picked a better time to walk in here and want a new truck. We were trying to meet a quota for this month, and today is the last day, and it's about 30 minutes until closing time."

He also said he'd give me a good deal that I wouldn't believe. He wanted $23,000 for it, and that's how I bought a new truck.

Now I had to figure out what I was going to do with the Ford truck. The truck still looked good; it just needed a motor. I worked with a guy, I'll call him Ralph for the sake of privacy, who had a garage. He could do anything mechanically. When I talked to him, he said, "If you can get a motor...I will change it for you."

I figured since I worked with the guy every day that he would treat me right. Also, he said he was a Christian, so I figured I didn't have anything to worry about.

My brother Danny told me that another mechanic had a thunderbird car he wanted to sell that had a 351 engine just like my truck. He said the car was in good shape and the engine sounded good. He wanted $800 for the car. I ended up buying it without going to look at it. I just gave Danny the money to pay the man.

I told the man to change the motor and that he could keep the thunderbird. We got the vehicles to his garage. I never asked him what he was charging me for the job. I had always believed that a man's word was as good as a contract. Wrong.

He finally got the truck done and I went to pick it up. I asked him what the bill was, and he said $1,300. He said he had to change all the gaskets on the engine. I figured I would drive the Ford and not put a lot of miles on the new Dodge.

It wasn't long until I saw some oil spots on the ground under the truck. I told him about it, and he said to bring it up and he would look at it.

Surprisingly, he said it was okay. I've always believed that if you do someone wrong it will come back to haunt you. I've had people to tell me all my life that you don't charge enough for what you do, my response was always: when I lay my head on the pillow at night I don't lay there and wonder about all the people I'd done wrong.

This guy ended up getting a divorce, lost his garage and got fired from work for stealing. God takes care of his children.

*****

I loved the new Dodge, but it only had a six-foot bed, and you couldn't haul a long ladder on it. So, I went back to Shelor's, and I ended up trading trucks and got another new Dodge.

I got a 2002 Dodge 2500, white with an 8-foot bed. I've still got it and it's now 20 years old. They gave me $23,000 for the quad cab. If I had to do it over again, I would have kept the quad cab and bought a trailer long enough to haul my ladders.

Chapter 28:
Major Life Steps

Allen and Julie decided to get married, so they had the ceremony at a church in Blacksburg. About a month later, John and Jamie got married at Faith Temple in Pearisburg. I walked her down the aisle and it was hard to keep from crying. She was our baby girl.

They got a house to rent over on Hopkins Street, also known as "High School Hill". The day they moved their stuff out of the basement I became sick. I guess I got a virus and was throwing up all day long. John had to get a neighbor to help him. I hated that so badly.

Jamie and John really wanted to buy a house though, so we looked at one that Lois Tabor had for sale. Lois was a good friend of mine who I had known for many years. The house was on the next street over. It was nice and had been remodeled from a garage to an apartment. She wanted $60,000 for it. They decided they wanted it and applied for a loan. They got the money they needed and were soon ready to move.

I could help John and Jamie with the move this time. I had made them a big China hutch for the dining room. It was made from one piece of red oak, which turned out to be a mistake. I didn't know I was going to move it two or three times. They later gave it back to me and I cut it into two pieces.

John had a big yard to mow. Carolyn's nephew had a Craftsman riding mower he wanted to sell, so we bought it, and left it on their porch. John was surprised when he came in from work and saw it.

One night my phone rang at about 2 am. John's youngest sister had wrecked in West Virginia. She was dead. They had called John, but no one answered the phone. They wanted to know if I could get a hold of him.

I left the house and walked over to John and Jamie's place. It was cold and snowing. I pecked on the door for what seemed like forever, but couldn't get any response. They had a slot in the door for the mail. I knelt there and began to yell. I finally got them to come to the door. It's awful to have to bring someone that kind of news in the middle of the night. I went to the wake and the funeral. It was a rough day.

******

I continued to work at my house and watched the workers until they got the concrete down. Then one day, Carolyn wanted to go to Walmart in Pearisburg, so I told the contractor to help himself with drinks or snacks in the refrigerator and I would be back in an hour or so. When we got back, I asked him how it was going. He said, "we have a small problem".

The stairs did not set up properly from taking the forms off too early and it made a bulge in the steps. I told him I didn't see how something like that could happen. The concrete people like to pull the riser on steps so they could know there were no places in the concrete. It had cooled down after dark, and it wasn't warm enough to dry the concrete.

He shouldn't have pulled the forms. He apologized but it was too late. I had to take a grinder the next day and spend all day grinding the steps so I could put carpet on them. You can't get anything the way you want unless you do it yourself. I should have made him break it out and re-do them, but I didn't let him know how I felt. Instead, I gave him a $50 tip.

Chapter 29:
The Robbery

I came in from work one evening and went upstairs to put my work clothes on. I walked into my bedroom, and I saw a couple of quarters lying on the floor. I didn't remember dropping any money; however, I did have a big jar of quarters under the desk that I was saving for Terrance.

I looked at the jar, and almost all the quarters were gone. I thought to myself how it could be that anyone came in here because I had a dead bolt on the door. I had all kinds of thoughts running through my head.

I thought about Julie buying painkillers, so I got to the phone and called her and directly asked if she took money from my bedroom. She said, "I can't believe you even asked me that." I said sorry but I had to rule out everything. Then I went to Carolyn and asked if anybody was there that day. She said David came by to see Terrance.

She also said he went upstairs to use the bathroom.

I asked how long he was upstairs but by then she was on a call and so she didn't remember. Then I remembered that I had a spare key for the bedroom and kept it on the top of the door. What happened to the money was now clear to me.

I called David and I told him I had to talk to him that I would be in the shop that evening waiting. I changed clothes and went there. It wasn't long until he pulled up.

He got out of his vehicle, and I just asked what I wanted to know. Surprisingly, he said he did it. I told him "I admire you for being honest, but I have been better to you than a father would be. You have known me long enough to know when I tell you something, I mean it."

He replied that he knew. I pointed my finger at him, and I made him a promise. "Boy, if you ever take another penny from me, I'll drop you. And I expect every penny of it back"

The exact amount of money he took totaled $860. He said he needed the money for a set of tires. He paid it all back, but to me, he was stealing money from his son. Carolyn and I were caring for his son, Terrance.

I don't know how he carried that many quarters out of the house. Only a thief would check over your doors to see if there was a key. I could never trust him after that. I still let him come to see Terrance, but I kept an eye on him.

Chapter 30:
Dark Times

As I continued finishing the house remodeling, I needed additional help. I asked my brother Danny and Elmer Fleeman to help me put the roof on the front porch and set the big columns-12 inches on the bottom and 10 inches on the top. I changed all my windows by myself in two days.

Allen was hired by me to clean up the mess. I went to Lowe's and bought a nice door for the front made of glass and two side lights. I put most of the siding up by myself, with a little help from John.

It was now well into the football season, but I couldn't stop to watch the games. I wanted to get the house done before winter arrived.

Terrance helped me to put the carpet down on the porch over Thanksgiving weekend. One Sunday, I put the bottom set of rails on the steps and there was snow on the ground.

I had put over $50,000 dollars into the house and still had to go back to the Credit Union to borrow more money. I traded my red Chevy van for a new Ford Expedition, really putting myself in debt.

*****

It was during this time that Julie was getting worse. She was taking Xanax and painkillers for her back.

One day, she and Cambria were going somewhere in Allen's little red truck. She was leaving the trailer park and pulled out in front of a car. It tore Allen's truck all to pieces.

Fortunately, neither one of them were hurt. There was a high drop-off on the other side of the road. If they had been knocked over the roadside railings, it would have probably killed both of them.

I had been thinking about Terrance starting karate. He was five years old now, so I figured it was time to enroll him. I took him to Pearisburg each time where he had classes two nights per week. He was really excited at first but then he wanted to quit. He kept wanting to quit, but I told him that he was going to go until he got his black belt. I was trying to teach him a little about responsibility. He didn't say much about wanting to quit anymore.

*****

Carolyn's brother, Bob, was told he was going to have triple bypass heart surgery. They did some tests and found out that he had cancer in one of his kidneys. The doctors also said they needed to take his kidney out before they could do the bypass.

He needed someone to stay with him and his wife, Jesse. Jesse wasn't in good health either. Previously, she had a lot of surgeries on her arm and leg. They talked to Julie, and she agreed to stay with them.

Joyce was going to pay Julie to stay and give her a check. She came to my house on Friday evening and wanted me to cash the check. I told her I didn't have enough money on me to cash it, so she said she would just take it to the credit union.

She called Carolyn that night and told her she cashed the check and that she was going Christmas shopping the next day, which was a Saturday. Carolyn and she were on the phone until about 12 am. During their conversation, she said she didn't know if she was going to be able to take care of Bob. Carolyn told her that she had already taken the money from Joyce, and she knew she had already spent most of it.

They hung up, but a little while later Julie called back again. Carolyn didn't answer the phone. I was upstairs in the bedroom and Carolyn had stayed downstairs on the couch.

It was December 14th, at 5:30 am, when I woke up and heard Carolyn screaming at the top of her lungs. The first thing I thought of was someone had broken into the house and was hurting her. I broke into a dead run down the steps and when I got there, she was jumping up and down screaming.

I finally got to her, and she told me that Julie was not breathing. I grabbed my wife, pulled her into my arms, and just held her. Allen had called and told her he didn't know what to do. I called him back and told him to call 911. They had a neighbor take Cambria next door and she watched them take her mommy out on the stretcher.

Allen explained later how he discovered Julie that morning. When he woke up, Cambria was in his bed, and that she had never done that before. I figured Cambria had woken up and found her mommy and it scared her. When Allen went into the living room, he found Julie slumped over on the couch.

He said when he went to bed that night, she was sitting on the couch counting her money. This was the worst feeling I have

Terrance and Cambrea at the time of Julie's death

ever had. I felt like part of me had died with her. I figured she had overdosed.

I had told her so many times about buying medicine from individuals. At this point, I didn't know the whole story.

After they took Julie's body out, they had to send her to Roanoke for an autopsy. Allen came to our house with Cambrea. He sat in the living room all day and never mentioned anything about making any arrangements.

Finally, I asked him if he wanted me to see about taking care of her burial, and he said he would appreciate it. I called an undertaker I knew and asked him if there was any way he could put her away and let Allen pay for it by the month. I had known the undertaker all my life. He said what we needed to do is to let the county put her away. I told him that I had just spent $50,000 on my house and I had two vehicle payments. I only said, "thank you and I'm sorry I even bothered you".

I called Eddie Kendall and told him the situation. He told me to bring Allen over the next morning at 9 am and they could talk. When we got there, he told us to pick out whatever we wanted. He said not to worry about how we were going to pay, as long as you make a payment every month, that it didn't matter how much, just to pay something.

We had her funeral at Faith Temple with Jeff Ray presiding. It hurt. As a father, you are not supposed to have to bury one of your children.

At the end of the funeral before they closed the casket, the pastor asked if anyone wanted to see her a last time before closing the top. I got Terrance in one hand and Cambria in the other and we went up to the casket. I bent over and kissed her goodbye on the cheek.

After the funeral, Carolyn's brother came to me and said the kids wouldn't have taken it as hard if I had not shown so much emotion. I thought to myself, Big Boy, you never had to lay one of your kids to rest. I didn't say anything. Some people don't think before they speak. Brother Ray Furrow told me a long time ago that before you say anything run it through your mind first because after you say it, you can never take it back.

Allen had her funeral paid for in less than a year.

Julia Dawn Perdue Cole
December 10th, 1970-
December 14th, 2003

Chapter 31:
Searching for Answers

It wasn't long before I started finding out more about Julie's death. Allen said that on Friday evening after Julie cashed the check, she went to see a woman, who I will call "Susan" in this context. She sold Julie some methadone. Julie had never taken that junk before as far as I knew. Susan and my sister Violet rented a house from Carolyn's sister.

One night, a few months after her death, Carolyn, Jamie and Crystal (Violet's girl) went out there to see Susan. They asked her about the methadone. When we got the autopsy results, it said her death was because of an overdose of that drug.

We did some research and found out that when you take methadone, your body stores some of it and it doesn't go away like it would with other pain killers.

Susan finally admitted that she had sold Julie the methadone. They had two investigators supposedly working on the case. I don't think they were working on anything concerning Julie.

Later that winter, Violet and Susan had gone to UVA hospital to stay with Jesse, my younger brother's stepdaughter. She had a brain aneurysm and wasn't doing very well.

Violet called me and wanted me to go check her house to make sure the heat was working okay. I had a key to the house because I looked after the property. When I went in, I did something I had never done before nor have I since; I pulled the drawer on a nightstand open, and it was full of pill bottles. Several of them contained methadone.

I called the investigators and told them. It was just a waste of breath. I about worried them to death calling them to see what they were going to do.

*****

Later that summer I was on vacation, and I got a call from the sheriff's department. The person on the phone said that I had a meeting scheduled with the sheriff at 1 pm. I told them I would be there. I had never met the sheriff; I told Carolyn that maybe they're finally going to do something about Julie's death.

I went into the meeting and the sheriff stood up and introduced himself. His father lived right below me on the next street down and was an engineer with Celanese. I worked with his father for years.

The sheriff looked at me and said they weren't even going to question Susan because the State of Virginia doesn't want the liability of taking care of her. She was already on Medicaid, which paid for the drugs she was selling. Of the two investigators that were sitting there that day, one died, and the other one got cancer.

I told them that when I lay my head on the pillow at night, I don't think about who I screwed over during the day. I got up and walked out. The sheriff's dad had always been very friendly with me, but after this day, he never spoke to me again.

I started calling the Drug Enforcement Administration (DEA) in Roanoke. I figured if anybody would do something that maybe they would. I called them at least once a week for a year. They acted like they were investigating the case and told me that every time they called the sheriff in Pearisburg, they would tell them to forget about it.

I had so much hate for the woman I felt was responsible for my daughter's death that I could hardly stand it.

Several years before Julie's death, a new convenience store opened in Pearisburg named Chubby's. I entered a raffle that the store conducted. The prize in the raffle was a one-year supply of gas equaling about 20 gallons a week for a year. Susan was one of the three managers at the store during that time. Someone stole about $13,000 from the store.

My son-in-law's brother worked there too, and he called me one night and said, "Guess who won the gas." What he told me next, I didn't believe. "I was with them when they drew the name out of the box, and it was Richard Perdue."

It went on for about two months that they never announced the winner. I got a guy I worked with one day to call Chubby's, the convenience store that held the contest, and ask who won. He also told them that if they do not announce who won he would put an article in the newspaper.

They said the winner was someone from Narrows, but they didn't want to say the name at first. This guy asked again, and they said my name. My workmate said, "Richard is standing right here. I'll let you talk to him."

They said they were going to get the certificates printed and they would call me back. I finally got the gas, but I always figured they were trying to make up for what was stolen from them. They probably knew one of the managers had taken the money. They all said they didn't know who took the money, but I would think the managers were the only ones with access to the cash.

Later on, there was another woman that Susan was staying with, and she died from an overdose of drugs. I called the town officer and told him I had some information about Susan. He just said, "I am the investigator of the case, and it is closed."

Chapter 32:
The Apology

The loss of my daughter and the events that led to her death just about drove me nuts! One day I made God a promise, that the next time I ran into this woman I would apologize to her. I needed to be free from the burden I was carrying. No one knew about this, only God and me.

The next night, I took Carolyn and Cambrea to Walmart. On our way back I passed Grant's supermarket in Narrows. Carolyn said she wanted something from there. I saw no problem, so I went around the block. She and Cambrea could go and get what they wanted, and I'd just wait for them in the vehicle.

When they came back, Carolyn said, "you will never guess who is in the store…Susan."

I said, "I'll be right back." I got out of the van and walked towards the store. There at the door in a handicap parking space was that woman, putting groceries in her trunk.

I could see the worried look on her face as I approached her. I told her "Susan, I've got to tell you something. I've had some bad thoughts about you, but I forgive you. I don't hold anything against you."

She said, "you don't know what that means to me." I turned and walked away.

That was the hardest thing I have ever had to do.

Sometime later I was thinking about what I had done. It happened on the anniversary of the day Julie died. That was my confirmation that God was the one who caused me to do this. It was like a big load was lifted off my back.

*****

Allen gave Carolyn custody of Cambrea so she could go to the school in our district. He worked 12-hour shifts, and he couldn't take care of a little girl.

She was five years old when we got her. I figured we'd be better off to go ahead and adopt Terrance too. I got a lawyer to take care of the paperwork, and he suggested I get David to sign the papers even though he had given up his custody years before.

I talked to David, and he agreed to do it. Terrance was eight years old. We had him all his life but now it was official. I was ready to raise my second family.

We took Terrance and Cambrea to Pigeon Forge in June that year. They liked getting on the rides. It was a big adjustment for Cambrea; you could tell she missed her mommy. We also took them to Knoxville Zoo, and they enjoyed looking at all the animals.

**Cambrea
an avid dancer for many
years**

Chapter 33:
Workplace Woes

I was asked to work over one evening and agreed. We had an upgrade foreman: someone who fills in for our regular foreman who was on leave at the time and receives a nice paycheck for it too.

Our job was to change the bonnet gasket on four automatic valves. The valves contained hot steam with acid vapor. The system was locked out and supposed to be empty. We put our locks on the lock box, and the operator signed our paperwork.

When we got to the job, we found out that one of the men had gone over to the jobsite during the daytime and changed two of the gaskets by himself. The valves were twelve feet in the air, and we had to use the overhead crane to lift the bonnets out and hold them until we changed the gasket and then replace the bolts. I don't know how he did it alone. Someone had to have helped him.

The upgrade foreman had signed his gate pass and let him go home and we were working shorthanded. We got ready to start. One man to operate the crane, one on each side of the valve.

We hooked the crane to the valve and signaled the man on the floor to lift the bonnet. I was standing on a 12-foot ladder. When he lifted the bonnet with the crane it blew, revealing it was under intense pressure. When it blew the hot steam, acid gusted towards my face. My reflexes kicked in, and I rolled away from the vapor causing me to fall off the ladder, hitting the end of a vaporizer that was under me. It had insulation on it and broke my fall. The whole five-story building was filled with hot vapor. It was a miracle from God that it didn't melt me.

The operator watched in horror. The man on the floor running the crane grabbed a water hose and began soaking me, fearing I was burning from the hot vapor.

The upgrade foreman told me to go to the shop and sit down and not to do anything the rest of the night. I went to the cafeteria and ate supper then went back to work and finished what we started.

I didn't go to medical check because I knew that at least two people would get fired, maybe more.

The guy that went home came to me the next day and said he heard about my fall last night. He did not mention the reason I didn't go to the clinic, and I am not sure if he thought about it. I knew God was still watching over me. He wasn't through with me yet. I was still alive.

If employees were involved in an accident, it seemed my employer would do everything in their power to fire you. I did not want to risk losing my job.

It took about six months before I got over this fall, both mentally and physically. When I later looked again at the jobsite where this near miss happened, the realization of how I could have survived looked impossible. There were a lot of people, like me, who got hurt and suffered silently to keep from losing their jobs. In every way you look at this accident I should have died.

When I write about all the times that God saved my life, I am also referring to the stress my Lord supported me through. I worked two jobs but also had a lot of problems happening personally. Struggles that I know God held my hand through and showed me the right path.

Another struggle I had was smoking cigarretes. I had always gone into the bathroom stall at work and smoked out of respect for the ones that didn't. I had a pastor 30 years ago that told me not to smoke in front of anybody in the church. I had tried to stop smoking but couldn't. I would throw them away in the evenings and be in the weeds the next morning looking for them.

One day, I went to the bathroom stall in the back of the building, to my typical spot. After shutting the stall door, I immediately noticed a written message. Someone had used a black marker to write, *Richard, everybody knows you smoke here*. As soon as I saw that God spoke to my mind and told me who had done this.

We always had a safety meeting before work in the mornings when the foreman would assign jobs. I asked my foreman if I could have the floor to speak after he was finished. I had something I wanted to say.

He let me have the floor, and I said, "One of you got something on me." I was one of the oldest men in the shop. I continued saying "God knows my heart and the reason I go back there to smoke, which is out of respect for the fact that some of you are offended by someone smoking. God showed me who wrote that on the door, but I don't really care about what you think. I just wanted to let you know that what you did doesn't bother me."

When they dismissed the meeting, I walked back through the shop. The man God told me was the culprit walked up and said to me that he hoped I did not think he was the one. I just told him that God knows all, and that was the important thing. I felt that he told on himself when he said that.

Chapter 34:
Calling me Back to Him

Carolyn came to me one day and asked me if I cared if she let Cristy, the babysitter, stay with us for a while. She had tended to children for most of her life. After she graduated from high school, she went to North Carolina and stayed with her daddy for about a year. She decided to come back, as she couldn't get along with her stepdad. She wanted to live with us for a while until she could find her own place.

I told Carolyn I wasn't going to make that decision but whatever she decided I'd be fine with it. She told her she could stay so she moved into the bedroom upstairs.

At this time, I had been thinking about getting my tattoos highlighted. I had one on each forearm. I went up to Princeton and looked around for the right place. I found a tattoo parlor who said they could do the work I wanted. It hurt more this time when they reinked my tattoos. When I first got them, I was in the marine corps at Ocean Side, California, and drank a fifth of liquor before making the decision.

After I got home, Cristy said she had some ointment that she used on her tattoos to keep them from getting sore. I used some of her medicine, but after a few days, my arms started breaking out around my tattoos. I figured that the tattoo parlor had exposed me to some kind of bacteria. Looking back now, my perspective has changed a bit. I think using Cristy's ointment on my tattoos may have caused the growth of bacteria. I should have known better, but sometimes things happen for a reason.

I went to my family doctor, and he put me on an antibiotic. That didn't work so he put me on a different kind of medicine, and it didn't work either. I went back again, and he then made an appointment for me to see a dermatologist. The dermatologist prescribed a different antibiotic. He asked me if I wanted them to do an upper body check since I was already there. So, he took a biopsy of a place on the right side below my mouth, another one on the back of my left shoulder and another place on my arm. The doctor said they were going to send those to the lab, and we should have the results back in about ten days. I had always wondered about how you would feel if they ever called and told you that it was cancer.

Those ten days passed, and one day at work, someone called me on the P.A. system letting me know I had a phone call. When I picked up the phone, the New River Dermatology office was on the other end of the line. The woman said the lab results were complete.

"The one he took off your arm is benign, and it was nothing to worry about, but the one by your mouth is cancer and it will require surgery. The spot on your shoulder is melanoma. He wants you in here for surgery as soon as possible," the doctor's office staff member said.

I didn't want to wait, and I asked if it was possible to go on that very same day.

It was two days before the surgery could be scheduled, and my appointment required me to arrive at 4 pm. I was prepped for surgery; then the procedure started. It felt like they stuck me about fifty times.

Each time they stuck the needle in my body, they went a little deeper. The melanoma was just sitting on top, and the roots never had grown down into my shoulder. I realized this was another miracle because I would have never gone to a dermatologist if not for the tattoo infection. Once the melanoma's roots grow down in you, it's hard to get rid of it.

I went to work the next morning and when my foreman saw me, he asked what happened. I ended up telling him and told me not to leave the shop that day, that I shouldn't have gone to work.

On the right side of my face where they had conducted the surgery, they had put glue on the cut. After you have had surgery for melanoma you worry a lot until you find out for sure that they got it all.

I started thinking about myself and decided I would feel better if I was in church. We hadn't gone to church anywhere for a while. I told Carolyn that in the next few days I was going to church somewhere but I didn't know where I wanted to go.

On that next Sunday, she suggested we go that night so we attended Faith Temple. She told me to drive my truck, and she would take the Expedition in case she didn't want to stay for the whole service.

My sister's girl had been talking to Carolyn trying to get us to come back to Faith Temple, so we felt comfortable going there. When we got to the church, the parking lot was empty. I told Carolyn that I didn't think they were having service that night.

It was then that I saw the pastor and Dwane coming down through the parking lot. Crystal had brought the Pastor down to the house while I had been gone to Walmart. He was there when I came back, and I met him. He had invited us to come back to the church.

I explained how we had come to Faith Temple and that I had surgery two days ago for melanoma. He asked if we wanted to go into the church and I said that would be okay. He told Dwane to go and get their wives, and he went inside and prayed. There are times when we get lax and we need to pray and do the first works over again. When we get in that place, Jesus Christ is always there with outstretched arms.

I had an appointment to go back and get my stitches out. It was a Wednesday; the nurse came in to remove the stitches and she said they had the lab work back and it was good. They had removed all the cancer.

She asked me if I smoked so I answered I did. Then she said I shouldn't do that. I went to church that night and I went to the altar. Down on my knees, I said, "Lord, you know my heart, you know what a time I have had trying to quit these cigarettes and now I give them to you because I can't do it. These things have me under their power".

That was fourteen years ago, and I have never wanted another cigarette. It was around the same time of my cancer scare that my son-in-law's aunt was also diagnosed with melanoma, but she didn't make it.

It wasn't long until the Pastor gave me the job of leading all the services. I always went to the Lord in prayer before the service and the Lord would always give me a scripture to read.

Sometimes the preacher would change his sermon, according to the Lord's Will. I remember one time we had an evangelist, and I opened the service and read a scripture. This visiting minister said that the Lord changed his message after I read my verse of scripture. The Lord was blessing every service, using me as a vessel. I was just a born-again child of God.

We had a praise team that sounded as good as any team in the country. My daughter Jamie was part of the team, and she is a talented singer. Her voice was just like the famous performer, Allison Krauss. I heard a DJ one day who said there are some people who can sing and there are others like Allison Krauss that have the voice of an angel.

Most nights, especially on Sundays, God's power really came down. People were slain left and right. There were young kids and teenagers lying all over the sanctuary. The services were like I remembered back in the 70's when we were first saved.

I really felt like God was going to do a great work.

Chapter 35:
A Heavy Load to Bear

It was time for Terrance to take his test for a black belt in karate. I had never gone in to watch him because I didn't want to distract him, but this night I wanted to be there. I recorded it all and it was something to see.

Terrance-Karate

The test took about two hours, and I was really impressed. I put him in karate because I wanted him to be able to defend himself. It was something to see for a young boy to defend himself from two adult black belts coming at him with knives.

I had told him for five years that he could quit if he wanted to. I figured that by the time he got his black belt he would want to stay.

They wanted him to be an instructor, but he walked away. I couldn't say anything. I tried to encourage him to stay but I had given him my word and keeping it was more important. When he got his certificate, black belt and suit, he put it in a drawer in my bedroom.

He knew Papa kept his word.

Terrance received his Black Belt in Karate after five years of training

We let Terrance go to his dad's trailer on Saturday nights and watch pay-per-view wrestling. He liked that. One night I took Terrance and Cambrea to Roanoke Civic Center to watch RAW and it was airing on television as well. I had always told David that he was welcome to see Terrance anytime he wanted and also gave David work from time to time when I needed help installing cabinets.

One Saturday night when Terrance came back from watching wrestling with his dad, he told me that David was dropping his potato chips on the floor all night. He said he got up one time, peeped around the door, and saw David sniffing pills. He never spoke to his dad again. David called here several times and wanted to talk to his son, but Terrance refused.

We were coming back from Walmart one day and Carolyn's cell phone rang, It was David's brother and he said that they found David dead. We were shocked. Terrance had lost his mother at five years old and now at thirteen, he loses his daddy. What a heavy load for a thirteen-year-old boy to deal with.

Carolyn called the pastor, and he came to our house. The pastor went up to Terrance's room to talk to him. It had really hurt him when he saw his dad with the pills.

I got the pastor to go with me, and we went up to his sister's house. I told them not to worry about the funeral; I was going to take care of everything. I told the pastor when we left that I thought I would at least get a thank you. He said that it was awfully nice of me. I told him that is why God blesses me so I can bless someone else.

We gave him a first-class funeral. We bought his tombstone and paid for everything. It's sad; I don't think anyone ever puts any flowers on his grave.

One of the town police officers in Pearisburg told me one day when I saw him at Walmart that they had received David's autopsy back and his death was due to an overdose of painkillers. Now Terrance would know that he lost both his mom and dad to drugs. Today, Terrance will not take any kind of pill. That's quite a burden to carry around in life.

Chapter 36:
Building the Cross

One Sunday morning I was sitting in the sanctuary and looking at the pulpit. There was a cross that someone had made hanging on the rocks in the front. When the pastor was there, he had the stained windows taken out and replaced them with obscured glass. I asked them not to throw the stained windows away because there are so many uses for them. One of the other deacons told me the pastor said to throw the windows away, but he kept them, and they are in the storage building. I guess the pastor wanted to make sure I did not get the windows.

I told some of the women what had happened. A few days later, my phone rang three different times, and the callers said they had stained glass windows and to come and get them. Eventually, I had all of them.

Sitting in the church that morning looking at the cross, it was like a big picture of a three-dimensional cross came through the wall and moved from west to east across the sanctuary. When it reached me, it paused for a few minutes. Then it started to move again and went out the other wall.

The following week, I continued to think about what I had seen. I told Carolyn about the experience and that I didn't know, but maybe God wanted me to build a cross. I went back to church the next Sunday and the cross was gone. I had told Carolyn there was a cross already in its place and didn't want to do anything to hurt anyone's feelings or make someone mad.

I asked one of the deacons what happened to the cross and he said it fell off the wall the previous week and broke into pieces. On my way out of the church that morning, I told the new pastor what had happened. She said the only thing she could tell me is to build a new cross.

I took off from work for three days and started working on my new project. Afte five hours had passed, things were not progressing well. I went into the house and got a cup of coffee. I said to Carolyn, "That cross can't be made;

there is nothing going right." She responded that I had never given up on anything as long as we had been together.

I went back to the shop and started cutting materials. Soon, things began to fall into place. The cross I constructed was absolutely beautiful and made from red oak. I designed the cross with the middle intersection of the beams wider and gradually thinning in width toward each point. The cross was five feet tall, and I added a light behind it. The frame made it look like it was suspended in the air with nothing providing support.

This is the stain glass that the pastor didn't want me to get my hands on, and the cross still hangs in the church today. Thank you, Jesus!

A police lieutenant I knew came by the shop one day and I showed him pictures of the cross I made. He said I should post the cross image on the internet and would get orders from everywhere. I just responded to the officer that I had more to do now than I could get done.

It was also during this time that Carolyn was getting to the point she didn't want to go out as much as she previously had. She preferred to stay home but didn't like being there alone. Most of the days when I left for work, she would leave in the Expedition and just ride around the streets close to our house or sit in Jamie's driveway. I could not imagine what it would be like to sit in a vehicle all day.

I recall in the '90s, I sat in the psychiatrist's office with Carolyn. The doctor told her he needed to get her off of the Xanax prescription she was taking, or she would be a basket case in twenty years. She replied, "I'm not worried about twenty years from now. I'm worried about today."

When Dr. Gillispie retired, I had to take her to another psychiatrist in Salem, Virginia. She was afraid to ride on the interstate by then.

Terrance was also playing football when the doctor found something out of order with his heartbeat. They sent him to see a heart specialist in Radford, and then to a specialist in Roanoke. His appointment landed on the day of a game. Terrance and I were in Roanoke almost all day. When the doctor finally approved him to play, we didn't think we were going to make it back before the team bus was supposed to leave. Terrance called someone on the team, and they held the bus until we got there. When the players saw us pulling in, they started clapping and yelling. He was one of the best players on the team.

Cambrea and I went to every Friday night game, whether it was home or away. Carolyn went to every home game, but she wouldn't travel. The first year we drove my Dodge 2500 truck. Boy, did it use a lot of gas!

John called me one day and said you need to see what I found on the internet. He was referring to a 2010 CTS with 20,000 miles and still under warranty. The car was located in southern West Virginia, in a town called Coeburn. The owner wanted $25,000 for it. I spoke with the owner and let them know I was coming to look at it. John offered to drive me.

Terrance - High School Football, Senior Star Player

Before we left town, I stopped at the credit union and transferred $15,000 to my checking account, just in case I made the decision to purchase the car. When we arrived, I fell in love with it. I had never owned a CTS, so I financed the other $10,000 to pay for it.

John asked me, "Do you want me to drive it back?"

I said, "I believe I can handle it." And it drove like a dream. Carolyn loved it too.

I wanted to choose something special for the car's license plate. I told Carolyn that God had gave me this gift and I wanted to praise Him in return. The woman at the DMV office was our friend and went to the same church as us. I called her and gave her a few different sets of numbers and letters I was considering. She said she would do some research to see if those combinations were available and then call me back. I prayed and asked God to give me what he wanted on the car. In that moment, I suddenly knew what I would put on my plates, PRAY USA. It was a perfect choice for the times we were living in.

Of course, I had no way of knowing what bad things were going to be coming next. I praised the Lord, saying "To God be the Glory," and enjoyed my new ride. It was certainly a lot better going to ball games riding in the CTS compared to my big truck.

Chapter 37:
Human Capital

Work continued to reveal difficulties to me in the management of employee resources and support. A staff member at work came up with the idea that the company would accept a certain number of people per year to include in corporate profit sharing. All employees could receive an annual percentage of the company's profits, but with this new program, the company would take a percentage back from each department. Three people in our shop, selected from the top of the seniority list, "took part" in the program. I was one of them, and this made me angry.

I went straight to the maintenance department's top supervisor and shared my frustrations. He said that not only was he not involved in the decision-making, but he wasn't there when it was decided who would be selected for the program. The foreman had been at a Virginia Tech bowl football game in Florida and would later resign because of this.

To show my anger, I used a black marker to write things about that deal on my white hard hat. Along with others, I was invited to a meeting with human resources. I wore my hat and sat close to the front of the room. I could see the head of the HR department stretching his neck to read what I had written on my hard hat.

Around September of 2012, I was checking equipment for any malfunctioning, like a bad bearing or other needed repairs. It was about 1 pm when I went to look through a hole in the side of a bucket elevator. To see the belt inside, I needed to get about a foot higher. This was a routine inspection that I had completed many times. Typically, a ladder was there for me to use, but that day it was missing. An antique high jacker was setting there instead and I only had to move it a couple of feet to step up on it. I just needed to raise up on the first step to see into the elevator. The cage was in the up position, so I reached up to pull it down when it fell, striking me in the head. The cage drove me to the floor. I was in so much pain, especially in my neck, that I could hardly bear it. Going to the medical office, I knew, could be disastrous as they would try to say it was my fault and maybe fire me. I was hurting so badly though, the fear of not going for medical care was more dreadful.

I went to the office and told the foreman what happened, and that I needed medical care. The foreman put me in the golf cart and drove me to the medical office. The medical team put me in a chair, packed my neck with ice, and gave me some ibuprofen, but did not send me to the doctor. I sat there for 3 ½ hours, and then they sent me home.

Terrance had a football game that night so one of the nurses at the game checked on me a couple of times. After looking at the high jacker, and how it was made, I believed somebody had intentionally meant to hurt someone or kill them by leaving it there.

The company did as I expected and tried to find fault in my accident. I discovered later that they were trying to set a precedent and, in the process, make the female plant manager look good. The company's goal had been to successfully achieve one million man hours without an incident. My neck was hurting terribly though. I was alternating Tylenol and ibuprofen every four hours and went back to the medical office multiple times, asking them to refer me to a doctor. At that time, I didn't know why but I kept records on everything that was said and every time I went to medical as well as my activities.

I met with my superintendent, and he said the accident was determined to be my fault and they couldn't find any malfunction with the equipment. However, he did tell me that if I had to take off from work, he would take care of me. I understood he meant that he would pay my wages if I needed to miss work due to my injury.

I continued to hurt. Repeatedly, I returned to the medical office, but they would just tell me that they intended to take care of me.

I spoke with the RN nurse in charge of my case. I had met her years before when I had to have a physical completed. She had left the company but then came back to work for them again. I asked her how she liked the company now. Her response was that she liked the job but not the things they make you do.

The pain became unbearable and exhausting to deal with. I decided to go to my family physician and request an MRI to see what was going on with my neck. I had also lost my sense of smell. I couldn't even smell a pole cat. The next day, I received the results and went to the medical office to tell them what had been found. The scans showed I had a bulging disc in my neck. The RN nurse was there and looked at the results and then called another nurse over. I shared what my doctor had told me again, but the nurse who had come over got a hateful look on her face and said it would be denied for a claim. It wasn't the nurse's fault. They were made to follow policy, and if they didn't, their job would end.

A letter from workers compensation came in the mail providing the date and time for a doctor's appointment in Wytheville, Virginia. I had to miss a day's work, but the doctor gave me some new information about my health condition. When the high jacker fell and hit me in the head, the doctor explained, it had severed an optic nerve in my forehead. I would always have trouble with my neck from time to time, he told me.

The doctor wrote a letter to the company stating that they needed to reevaluate their medical department. Workers' compensation decided to take it to court. My family doctor then sent me to see a neurologist in Roanoke. After reviewing the MRI they conducted, he prescribed therapy, which I was able to do at Giles Memorial Hospital.

I scheduled my therapy appointments to attend during work hours. The superintendent had told me to take care of myself following the accident, so I assumed it was okay to use work time for the therapy sessions. The appointments were twice a week for a span of ten weeks. This resulted in my time away from work to equal three hours each time I had therapy. The company docked my pay. At $25 an hour, the total income loss came to approximately $500, plus the cost of gas. Another $200 plus gas for my visit to Wytheville to see the neurologist. To this day, July 2022, ten years following the accident, my pain persists daily, and I have no sense of smell.

The next letter relating to my worker's compensation came in the mail. A hearing had been scheduled. I called around to a few lawyers in the Roanoke area who specialize in workers' compensation. The information each of them relayed to me was disappointing. According to them, in the state of Virginia, the employer typically comes out the winner in these cases, not the employee. The lawyer fees were going to be astronomical too, so I called the workers' compensation office and told them to drop the charges. She said you can't afford not to go, and I wouldn't have a leg to stand on. So, I made the unfortunate decision to represent myself. The union had not been supportive since the accident and had only accompanied me to a physical at the medical department. Their only purpose is to serve as a witness for information communicated during the initial medical evaluation.

On the day of the hearing, we arrived fifteen minutes early and found the appropriate room mentioned in the letter. A man was already in the room, and when we made introductions, I discovered he was the judge. The two of us chatted prior to the start of the hearing and I made it quite clear that I was a Christian and what I stood for.

Looking back, I can say the people I met that day was an experience that I will never forget. Representing myself was a mistake, especially against a Philadelphia lawyer. The nurse they called as a witness did not tell the true events as they happened either, even though she had taken an oath on the stand. I had kept a log of everything that had happened and gave that to the judge at the hearing's close.

The judge had 30 days to make his decision. The union brought in a corporate safety employee and she met with me two times; prior to the hearing and again after receiving the judge's decision.

Additionally, the evening of the hearing, the nurse texted my foreman to arrange a meeting about "Mr. Perdue" and what they were going to do about me. My foreman responded that he was through discussing Mr. Perdue.

The judge's decision came via a notarized document. I would not be reimbursed for any money I had lost from wages or doctor's appointments I had attended. The judge only said that if I had any problems with neck in the future, workers' compensation would take care of it.

In a second meeting with corporate safety, the woman asked me how I thought the outcome of the hearing should have been different. I gave her two names. These two men had done people wrong for years. She replied that it was time for both of them to go and in less than 30 days they were no longer employees at the company. I assumed they were given a buy-out or elected for an early retirement.

I headed straight for my superintendent's office and found him sitting at his desk. I said to him, "I thought you were going to take care of me?" He just shook his head and didn't say a word.

At this point in my life, I had two more years until I could retire at age 65. I thought to myself that surely, I can make it that long. My goal would be to do only what I had to do and no more, and I made sure that my foreman and everyone else I worked with knew this.

The safety department decided to do a display with everyone's handprints, signatures, and their time with the company. I had no interest in being a part of this project and declined to dip my hand in paint. When the display board was placed at the gate, a handprint bearing my name, signature, and my years of service to the company were on it. I was irritated and went straight to the superintendent's office to let him know how I felt along with wanting to also address the shop in the morning. The superintendent agreed to let me speak with them. The superintendent also wanted to know if I had an idea who would do something like that. I knew exactly who it was as God had already showed me. The superintendent asked for the person's name, but I refused to tell him. I told him that God would take care of them.

The next morning, I went to the shop floor and chewed the employees out. I told them this was a low blow and that God would deal with you. Upon leaving I walked through the shop and the one I knew had put my name and handprint on the board approached me from behind and denied the accusation, hoping I didn't think he was the one.

The superintendent came to me later that day and asked if I had found the culprit. I relayed the events of the meeting and what followed. Again, the superintendent asked me who it was, but I remained silent. Telling on the employee would have only created more trouble.

At the end of the meeting, my foreman asked if anyone had additional comments. I raised my hand and told the group that I would be retiring in two weeks. My foreman responded that my absence would be greatly felt by the company. I could feel it too after spending so much of my adult life working there. On the other hand, I was ready to leave.

Around October 3rd, I was able to get a gate pass and a couple of the other employees helped me retrieve my personal tools. I used a forklift to load some of them on my truck. The entire shop celebrated with a catered dinner for me.

On the last day of work, the clock was ticking along and my last couple of hours of work were approaching. One of my friends snuck up behind me and poured a bucket of water over my head. It was a wonderful tribute, because if they had not wet me down, I wouldn't have known they cared for me.

The first day of my retirement I began work remodeling a house next door. I had no idea about the problems that awaited me, as I had not told the company ahead of time that I would be retiring.

Chapter 38:
A Rocky Start to Retirement

The company had not relayed to the benefits office that I had retired. My retirement check from the company was delayed for an additional month. I called the human resources department every morning. In addition to my retirement benefits, they also owed me five weeks of vacation pay which totaled over $5,000, which I did finally receive. I asked a woman I knew to also call the life insurance company and confirm my benefits were in good standing. I was relieved to hear that they were. I didn't feel I could trust the company to look out for my welfare.

The exterior remodeling on the house I had started was completed in 30 days. Carolyn's sister had bought another rental house, so I had another house to remodel.

One day I was working on the rental house by myself. I had to cut a 1 ½-inch vent line to be able to pull the pipe out of the roof's overhang. Standing on a stepladder, I used a 4 ½-inch grinder to cut the pipe. I had almost cut into the pipe when the grinder binded and kicked back, hitting me in the hand and cutting my middle finger's tendon. When I looked at my hand, my finger was hanging down. I pulled a shop rag out of my pocket and used it as a wrap. I climbed down from the ladder, jumped in my truck, and sat on my hand to apply pressure.

Driving to the doctor's office at 80 miles per hour, I arrived and ran inside. I told them at the desk about my deep cut and need to see a doctor right away. She took one look at my hand and yelled for a nurse, who told me to head to the ER.

At the ER, a doctor evaluated me and then requested a surgeon to look at my hand too. I was told that surgery would be necessary, but it could not be scheduled for about a week, so they stitched it up.

I had to clean up my tools, so I returned to the house. The next day, I returned to working on the house, using only one hand, and continued that way for several days. My sister-in-law suggested telling my son-in-law what had happened, and he and another man from Georgia would pick up the work in my absence. I let my replacements know what had to be done and took three days off for my surgery. When I returned to the job, we installed a full bath and rewired the whole house. No one could believe that I had continued working on the house with my injury, but we got the job done. Due to the injury though, I still had to complete four weeks of therapy.

Chapter 39:
Prayer Warriors

The fall of 2017 started with a sore tooth. I figured it could wait until after the new year, and then I would go see about it. Jamie and John always cooked a lot for Christmas and the new year celebrations. I didn't want to miss out on the good food.

I scheduled an appointment for January 2nd, went to the dentist and told him my tooth was sore. He asked what I wanted him to do with it. I said, I guess you could pull it out, and he did, removing it easily. Never before had a tooth come out so gently.

My teeth cleaning appointment was coming up soon, so the dental office delayed the appointment for a couple of weeks to allow my mouth to heal from the tooth extraction. When I did go in the dentist's office again, my mouth was still sore and I told him so. After cleaning my teeth, the dentist thought an antibiotic might be necessary, so he prescribed one. But there was still no relief from the soreness in my gums. The dentist put me on another antibiotic. Still no resolution; still in pain, and there was a white appearance to my gums now.

I returned to the dentist again and he was able to get an appointment with a dental surgeon, but it would be some time before they could get me in to see the doctor. I called their office to request they put me on the cancellation list for a sooner appointment.

It was snowing that morning and so I didn't have to wait but 30 minutes until my phone rang; I could see a doctor in Radford. I told them I would be there. Then, I called my sister, Violet, and she said she would go with me.

When we arrived at the dental office and I met with the surgeon, he looked in my mouth. He would need to do a biopsy, he said, to know for sure what was wrong. I was willing to move forward right then, so the nurse came in to numb me up. She took pictures of my mouth too, and gave me a bunch of shots.

As the surgeon more closely inspected my mouth, he was upfront with the prognosis. He said it looks like cancer to me.

I didn't have any dental insurance, and told him I might have to suffer some and deal with the pain. It would be nothing like the pain that Jesus suffered on the cross at Calvary though, I shared with the doctor. The doctor said, man, I love your way of thinking!

The nurse told me later that the doctor would normally charge up to $1,300 for the procedure, but he only charged me $750.

The surgeon then sent the biopsy to Richmond to a dental college for processing. It was ten days later when I reported back to the surgeon's office for the lab results; the doctor was right, it was cancer.

No one can imagine what it is like to hear those words. The doctor said I would need surgery and he would be able to schedule something at Wake Forest or at the Lewis Gale Hospital in Salem, Virginia. We decided I would first go to Salem and then, if I wanted a second opinion, the surgeon would call Wake Forest for a referral.

When I arrived in Salem at Lewis Gale, Dr. Brian Gross, the nicest man I ever met, relayed to me how bad the cancer was. Then, he reached out his hand and said, can I pray for you?

Dr. Gross had to schedule the surgery and I had to get a full body scan to see how much of the cancer needed to be removed. I wanted to have the surgery completed as soon as possible, knowing the longer it remained in my body, the further it would spread.

After about a week, I had not heard any new information. I called the radiology office in Blacksburg and asked them if they were backed up or if they had some information as to when I would be scheduled for the scan I needed. They responded that once they received the order for the scan, they could do it anytime. Frustrated, I called the surgeon's nurse and told her I didn't want to wait! In two days, I had an appointment for a scan.

After the phone call confirming my appointment, I went upstairs and locked myself in the bedroom, kneeled down on a quilt, closed my eyes and raised my hands. I said, "Lord, you know my heart, and it's out of my hands. I'm asking you to take care of things."

I was sitting in my recliner, listening to southern gospel CD's and tears running down my cheeks when the phone rang. When I answered it, John, my son-in-law was on the line. He worked at the Church of God in Princeton and asked if I wanted to take a ride with him to the church. I agreed but didn't know what he had planned. When I walked into the church I was greeted by nine preachers. I was looking for a miracle and someone said I had come to the right place. I'm still carrying a prayer cloth in my billfold they used that day to anoint me.

Jamie got on the internet and told me that people around the world were sending up prayers for my healing, even as far away as Italy she once called to tell me. T.D. Jakes called me on the phone one day and prayed for me along with Francis Swaggert, who sent a letter with her church family's prayers.

There were times I felt sorry for myself, but God would always send someone along to cheer me up. The week before surgery, I remodeled a bedroom in the basement for Terrance. He wanted to move his bedroom down there. I was trying to catch up on everything because I did not know how long I would be recovering. I drove my truck to Pearisburg to have it inspected and was waiting when a man came in and set down next to me. He was the pastor of the Baptist Church located on my street of residence. He asked me how I was doing, and I told him about the impending surgery. After we talked a little while, he told me, "I'm not worried about you. You will be fine, but I will call you the day before and check on you."

The pastor did call, and Pastor Debbie Hutton also came by the house. She said she would stay with Carolyn on the day of the surgery, but my wife just wanted Jamie to stay with her. So, Debbie decided to come to the hospital instead.

The day came for my surgery and John took me to the hospital. I was escorted to the prep room where I removed my clothing and put on a hospital gown. The pastor then came into the room and prayed with me. Soon, the nurses came in and said it was time for me to leave the prep area but would allow John and the pastor to accompany me until the moment I was to go into the surgical room.

I lay in the bed waiting. The surgeon Doctor Gross and his assistant appeared and he asked, "Mr. Perdue, are you ready for your surgery?"

I told him I was excited so let's do it.

The doctor asked the pastor to lead us in prayer. We all joined hands, and she began to pray. What I felt in that moment was something I had never felt before, but I wouldn't trade for all the money in the world. I knew everything was going to be fine.

The medical team took me into surgery and explained how the anesthesia would be administered. That is all I remember until I woke up 7 ½ hours later in my hospital room. I felt different now. I had a thick pad sewed into the roof of my mouth with a drainage tube protruding out. It felt like there was a hole in the back of my mouth and throat the size of my little finger. They had pulled all of my teeth on the top left side and I had a drainage tube coming out of my neck.

The procedure required the removal of a skin graft from the top of my left leg and they had to bore a hole from the top of my mouth into the left side of my sinuses. They also removed all the lymph nodes on the left side of my neck.

The surgeon came in to see me and asked how I was doing. I responded okay, considering what I had been through. He told me I was the most phenomenal man he had every met. I raised my hand towards heaven and said, "It's not me, it's Him." He responded that he knew.

John called Carolyn and Paisley through the Facetime application, and I was able to talk to them. Paisely was so glad to see her Pawpaw.

Sleeping was scary for me; I was afraid I would cough up blood and choke. So, John and I watched Jimmy Swaggert all night on television.

The next morning, John asked me if I was ready to go to the bathroom and look in the mirror. I wasn't sure if I was ready to see what my face looked like after the surgery. It turned out not to be as bad as I expected. However, the worst part of my recovery was the food; everything I ate had to be pureed in a blender. I was still alive though, and I knew God wasn't through with me yet. Praise the Lord!

John stayed with me the whole time I was in the hospital. He was my guardian angel. He had the nurse's phone number and would call if I needed something. Granny (Carolyn) and Paisley were glad to see Pawpaw still kicking too. They would Facetime with me several times a day. Before I could go home, I had to walk the entire hallway two times, twice a day. It was tough the first time I did it, but John was right by my side. After the first trip, it got better. The doctor wanted me to go home after two nights, but I was still a little scared to leave. I asked if I could stay one more night and he said it was okay.

The people who were supposed to bathe me never came. One of the night nurses who took care of me was named Casey. It was around 11 pm one night when Casey came into my room. She asked if anyone had given me a bath and when I told her no, the nurse offered to give me one. I said it would be fine. Casey said she would return after catching up on her work, probably around 5 am. She also said, "I will wash everything, but you will have to wash your jewels." When I filled out the satisfaction survey before I left the hospital, I gave her an excellent rating.

The day came for me to go home. John pulled his car to the hospital door and I was pushed out in a wheelchair by the hospital staff. I knew this was only the beginning and I had a long road of recovery ahead. When we arrived home, I had never in my life been so happy to be there and see everybody. Paisley still tells me sometimes that I was crying. Jamie had put up signs and balloons welcoming me home.

John stayed with me for two days and nights, fixed my food, and took care of me. I knew taking care of myself was something I would need to do. I told John how much I appreciated everything he had done and how he had been my guardian angel. It was time I took care of myself though, so he went home. John still came back for several days to check on me.

For a while, I had to go back to Salem every week to see Dr. Gross. One morning I woke up and the pad sewed to the roof of my mouth had loosened and was hanging down across the entire front of my mouth. I looked in the mirror and said to myself, "What do you do now, Big Boy?" I located my small pair of pointed scissors and a magnified mirror and then turned on all the lights in the bathroom. I proceeded to cut the stitches so I could remove the pad from my mouth. Then I called the doctor to let him know what happened and that I needed him to look at my mouth. Both my sister Violet and my brother Danny went me to a lot of my appointments.

I was facing five years of doctor appointments. Dr. Gross sent me to a dental surgeon to look at my mouth and start rebuilding it. Danny went with me to the dentist too. The dental surgeon evaluated my mouth and took several x-rays. My mouth was still very sore and aching. I also didn't have any dental insurance at the time and the dentist didn't accept Medicare; however, he knew someone through a Carilion office who would, and they had an open appointment. I had to pay the bill out of pocket, and it came to about $400.

Carolyn called me while I was at the dentist's office. She said a woman she had babysat as a little girl called and wanted to borrow money, $40 to be exact, but Carolyn decided to give her $20, and she could pay back the other $20 at a later date. The woman borrowing the money had leukemia. So, Carolyn told her to come over and she would lend her the money she needed.

When the woman came to our house, Carolyn was outside by the van with Paisley. It was then that Cambrea called my wife on the phone. She wanted to take the call so she asked the visitor if she would mind watching Paisley while she talked. After the woman took the $40 and left, Carolyn looked into her purse and discovered that a total of $380 was gone. The woman had taken all of Carolyn's money.

We called the police, and they went to question the woman about the missing money. She admitted she stole it. To charge the woman with the crime of theft, the case would be heard in court. That would also mean Carolyn would have to appear in court; she received a subpoena. Carolyn was unable to go, and I went to the courthouse to tell them so. The case was never heard and the woman passed away. About a year later, the woman's husband passed away too. I learned that the woman had stolen money and other things from many different people.

Back at the Carilion dental office, they made an impression of my mouth so that an arbitrator could be made to cover the hole created from surgery. The space made from the surgery had left a gaping hole in my mouth to my sinus cavity, just below my left eye.

I was facing thirty treatments of radiation at the Pulaski Cancer Center, and I contacted them to schedule the appointments. I had seven different doctors to see. Some days, I would make two appointments: one in the morning for radiation in Pulaski and the other in the afternoon for the Roanoke office so they could fit me properly for the arbitrator. A contractor was building the arbitrator for my mouth, but it would not be finished until the radiation had ended. They also told me if my weight dropped to a certain level, I would need to have a feeding tube. I didn't want that to happen, so I forced myself to eat, even though I didn't feel like it.

About halfway through the radiation, I told Carolyn I wanted to stop treatments. I just couldn't take it anymore. I had a lot of headaches, so they sent me for a brain scan to make sure radiation hadn't gone into my brain. When you have cancer around your head, there are a lot of scans involved. After thinking about the radiation treatments, I decided not to quit, and I am glad now that I didn't.

One day, I was talking with Doctor McCool and he told me how surprised he was at my appearance. He said he couldn't believe I look as good as I did. I responded that I probably look a lot better than I feel.

At one point, they did a full body scan, and it showed I had spots in my head and on my left lung. In Pulaski, they did x-rays and a biopsy of my lung. When they pulled me out of the scans, the doctor had good news for me. The spot on my lung was breaking up and the doctor believed the spot in my head would break up too.

I could hardly wait to finish the radiation treatments. When the day arrived of my last treatment, I rang the bell in the hallway announcing my good news. It was a long time before I completely recovered from the radiation, if a person ever truly gets over it. I think in total, the radiation cost was $200,000. I asked the nurse one day what a person would do if they could not afford the treatments and did not have insurance. She said they don't get treated.

The next step would be reconstructing my mouth. They did a fitting for the arbitrator and then sent it back to Ohio for adjustments. It had to be perfect. I also went ahead and had a partial made for my bottom teeth, which I had to pay for out-of-pocket. Medicare paid for the arbitrator. They also made cups for my upper and lower teeth. I had to put fluoride in them every night and leave them on my teeth for ten minutes. Several times, they had to pull stitches out of the roof of my mouth because of me removing the pad that had come loose following surgery.

Finally, my arbitrator and partial were finished.

Carolyn was not doing good at all. Over a twelve-month period, I called an ambulance five times to take her to the Giles County Hospital's emergency room. All five times she had urinary tract infections (UTIs). She had also been saving Xanax over the years and was taking some of them, plus what the doctor prescribed her. Her doctors were trying to get her off the Xanax medication by decreasing the number of pills she was given with the goal of starting her on another drug. She had always been afraid of new medications.

One night, some of us were sitting in the living room and I started coughing and couldn't stop. Carolyn told Cambrea to call 911. The ambulance came to the house. As soon as I was given oxygen, I stopped coughing. The EMTs took me to the hospital's emergency room, examined me, but couldn't find anything wrong. They asked me if I had someone to drive me home. I told them no, but I guess I could wait until Cambrea's husband ended his shift at 7 am. I would then ask him if he could drive me home. The male nurse told me to lay down in the bed and go to sleep and he would wake me around 6 am. I could not sleep so about 5 am, I crawled out of the bed.

The nurse came in again and asked if I needed anything, but all I wanted was a big cup of coffee. Then, I went to the lobby and bought a cake from a vending machine. After about two hours, Zack showed up around 7 am and took me home.

Terrance started having trouble with his stomach and chest area. He went to the Pearisburg medical clinic and saw a nurse practitioner. She told him it was probably the food he was eating. He always did eat a lot of fast food. She put him on Prilosec, but he did not improve.

He finally went to Pembroke and saw a doctor from the Lewis Gale network. They did bloodwork, determining Terrance had leukemia. He was then referred to the Blacksburg Cancer Center.

As we pulled into the parking lot that day, he looked over at me and said at 23 years old, he never thought he would be going to a cancer center.

He was then sent to the University of Virginia (UVA) Medical Center in Charlottesville, Virginia, where he started a round of chemo. The cost was $35,000 a month. Fortunately, he held a job at Volvo and his insurance would pay everthing at the cancer center. That was three years ago and he is still on chemo treatments.

The Lord sent Terrance's little girl along to keep me going. She's Pawpaw's little baby doll; just a bundle of joy. She has also kept me busy just trying to keep up with her. I told her one day that my goal was to see her graduate from high school. I said, "Do you think Pawpaw will get to see you graduate?" She said, probably not.

Carolyn continued to get worse. One night she refused to take her medicine. She had already taken all the Xanax the doctor had given her. She was taking the new medication that she was supposed to take along with the Xanax, but she would not take it when I prepared it for her. I figured she was going through withdrawal.

I called 911 and they sent two cops to our house. The officers tried talking to her-convince her to take the medications. Carolyn told them that she wasn't going to take it because I might have put something in there that would kill her. The cops knew me and that I would never do anything to hurt her. One of them took me into the living room and the other one stayed in the kitchen. They were able to get her to take her medication. We had Paisley, and I was awake late that night. At that time, we were keeping Paisley about sixty percent of the time while her parents were both working.

The next day, Paisley and I were in the nursery. She was playing with her toys, and I was sleepy from not getting enough rest the night before. I guess I dozed off. I couldn't have been asleep more than ten minutes when I opened my eyes and she was gone. I jumped to my feet and ran to the kitchen. There was no one in the house and it was cold outside. I went back to the living room and Carolyn was coming in through the living room door. I said, "Where is Paisley?' Carolyn said she gave her to a woman. I asked her what woman she was talking about and she told me it was none of my business. I called 911 and told them I needed a police officer to come to our house right away. They said they would be there in a few minutes.

Paisley
Great-granddaughter

I then discovered that Carolyn had taken Paisley across the street to a neighbor's house and left her with the woman. The woman knew Paisley's mother, Kalyn, and she called Paisley's aunt to come and get her.

The town police officer arrived and asked Carolyn if she knew me. I opened my mouth to respond, but was interrupted by Carolyn. She was holding a 16 ounce bottle of Dr. Pepper in her hand and standing next to the cop. Carolyn looked at me and said, "If you open your mouth, I'll hit you between the eyes with this pop!"

The cop said, "Oh! No, no!" The officer called for an ambulance and told me we would need Carolyn's agreement to have an evaluation. If she did not consent, Terrance would have to go before the magistrate and sign papers. He told him we would if we had to, but when the ambulance arrived, Carolyn agreed to go. Her family doctor was contacted; he signed off on her transport to Saint Albans, a psychiatric hospital. Later that day, someone from the hospital called to say they would be keeping her overnight.

At 5 am the following morning, my phone rang. A Carilion staff member was calling to let me know the results of their examination. Carolyn had dementia and was in route to Dickinson County on the Kentucky border. I was told to wait about three hours until they had time to settle her in and then I could call and maybe speak with Carolyn.

Hearing this news broke my heart. God said He *would never put more on us than what we can bear*. There was a saying I recall from the Marine Corps too. *When the going gets tough, the tough gets going.* I knew God was also taking care of her.

I called about three or four times a day to check on her. They kept her nine nights in all. When I spoke with her, it sounded like all she had been doing was walking the hallways back and forth. She was probably looking for a way out.

Jamie called to inform the hospital about her mother's five UTIs and sure enough she had one at this time too. One night they also called me to try to talk Carolyn into going to bed. She refused to go to sleep, so I said I would try to calm her down, but it did not work. I could hear them tell

Zack and Cambrea (married)- Ocean City, Maryland

her three times that it was past bedtime, and she needed to quiet down. Then the phone disconnected.

Jamie called back to the hospital to see what had happened. They said she had to have a shot. Carolyn told me the next day she had a sore spot on her arm but couldn't remember where it came from.

The doctors at the hospital changed all of her medicine and it was soon time for her to come home. Jamie told them there was no way her daddy could drive her mommy home with the fits she had been throwing. They said they could give her something to calm her during the ride and would transport her home.

The day she was to arrive home, I had decorated the house and expected her anxiously at the time the hospital had given me. I put balloons all over the rails on the front porch and made a sign that read *Welcome Home Granny*. A big red ambulance pulled into the driveway. When she emerged from the vehicle, she looked like a whipped puppy. I felt so sorry for her. Sometimes we have to do things we don't want to do, but looking back, this was one of the best things I have ever done.

Since then, I have been taking care of her medicine, and she is doing well. I installed deadbolts on all the doors so she cannot get out of the house at night while I am sleeping. She went out on the porch one night and then came back in; she didn't know I was watching her.

I went to the dermatologist for my annual check-up. I had carcinoma, requiring out-patient surgery on the left side of my face and the back of my left arm above my elbow. This was the same type of cancer I previously had.

Last fall, I asked three three different doctors if I should have a covid vaccination. They all made the same recommendation that the vaccine would be a good idea because of my health history. I had two different cycles of the vaccination. In January, I contracted covid.

One day, I was taking the trash to the street to be picked up. This is a task I have been doing for 42 years. I stepped on a spot of snow, and my feet went out from under me. I landed on my back and couldn't move. The pain was so intense that I laid there for a while. I told myself 'you have to get up. There is no one to get you up.'

It wasn't easy to pick myself up off the ground that day. Later, I went to see a Veterans Administration (VA) doctor, and he sent me for x-rays and a MRI. I had 38% fracture on the bottom plate of my spine. I also messed up four discs in my vertebrae and have arthritis in my spine.

My grandson's girlfriend asked me what I was going to do now. I told her I was going to keep getting up. She then asked what I would do when I couldn't get up anymore. I replied, "I'm going home!"

I told Carolyn I hoped the Rapture would take place so we can go through the clouds together, holding hands. Praise the Lord!

Lord Jesus come quickly and take us home.

The Call

Where were you when God made the call?
Did you ignore the call or did you say
Yes Master, I'll take it all?
Did you feel you were unworthy to take the call?
We are all unworthy for the call,
But the grace of God covers it all.

You might have been in church
when you felt the draw.
You might have been running the ball,
Or felt you were running against the wall.
How many times have you
turned down the call?

God is almost ready to tell Jesus
Go and gather them all.
The next call will be silent
as we join Jesus in the air.
Do you know if you're ready?
Do not stall.

Jesus gave it all when God made the call.
Jesus went to the cross and
gave it all.
He rose on the third day
so he could save us all.

Carolyn and Richard, 52nd Wedding Aniversary

Richard, Paisley, and Carolyn

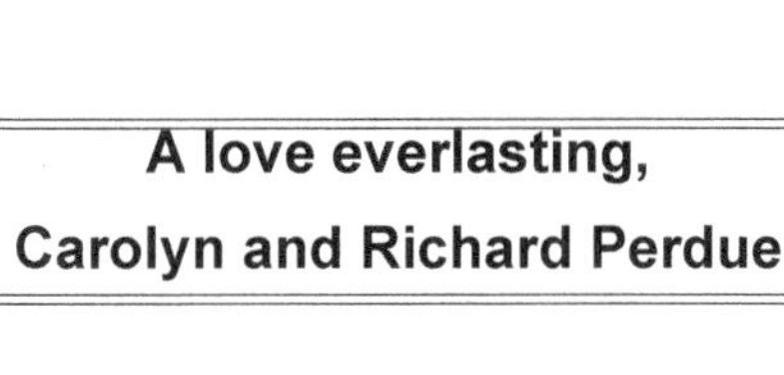

A love everlasting,
Carolyn and Richard Perdue

(below-right) The day Carolyn came home from the hospital.

Our house after remodeling